MONEY SKILLS FOR TEENS BLUEPRINTS

Unlock Financial Independence in Seven Easy Steps to Master Budgeting, Develop Saving Habits, and Manage Allowances Effectively

D. MCCLARENCE

Table of Contents

Introduction

Have you ever felt overwhelmed by the thought of managing your finances as a teenager? Do you find yourself wondering how to make your allowance last longer or how to crack the shell for that big purchase you've been dreaming of? Or do you feel the frustration of financial uncertainty? Well, many teens face the challenges of limited financial literacy, uncertainty about saving, inexperience with smart spending, and the elusive concept of financial independence. So, you're not alone, and don't take that as a consolation because …

This is the consolation—your trusted companion on a journey to transform those challenges into triumphs. Through our F.I.N.A.N.C.E. Blueprint, we'll unravel the seeming mysteries of budgeting, saving, and investing in a language that speaks to you—friendly, supportive, sympathetic, yet relentlessly practical. It's time to empower yourself with actionable strategies, real-world examples, and tools that not only guide but resonate with the unique financial needs of teenagers.

In the phase of teenagehood, where every dollar counts, the catalyst that brought you to *Money Skills for Teen Blueprint* is one that's intimately understood. It's the desire to wield your allowance with savvy finesse, stretching it to cover not just the basics but also those significant purchases that make the subsequent stages of adolescence memorable. Your catalyst is the drive to manage your finances with newfound wisdom, to save effectively for those coveted goals, and to make every spending decision an intentional trap toward financial independence (if it were a snare). This book isn't just a title; it's your beacon of hope, illuminating a path tailored to your unique needs. As you turn these pages, you'll discover practical guidance and actionable strategies, transforming your financial journey from a puzzle to a well-charted course.

Now, to the heart of *Money Skills for Teen Blueprint*, where the F.I.N.A.N.C.E. Blueprint unfolds, guiding you step by step toward financial independence. Each letter in this powerful framework represents a crucial aspect of your journey, offering insights and strategies tailored to the unique challenges and aspirations of teenage finance.

F – Foundation Building

In this opening chapter, we'll lay the groundwork for your financial journey. Here, we'll emphasize the importance of financial literacy and responsibility. You'll delve into the fundamental concepts of money management, gain insights into budgeting, and learn the basics of credit. Consider this section as the bedrock upon which your financial independence will stand— a solid foundation built on knowledge and practical skills.

I - Investment in Education

Moving forward, we'll transition to investment in education. This isn't just about stocks and bonds; it's about arming you with a comprehensive understanding of various financial concepts. From banking services to the importance of investing early for long-term wealth accumulation, you'll gain insights that go beyond the classroom. Think of this section as your crash course in financial wisdom, designed to empower you with the knowledge to make informed decisions about your money.

N - Nurture Smart Spending Habits

Next up, we'll dive into the art of smart spending. The focus here is on developing prudent spending habits by distinguishing between needs and wants. Through relatable examples and practical advice, you'll learn to prioritize spending on essentials and allocate discretionary funds wisely. This section is your guide to becoming a savvy spender, ensuring that every dollar you spend aligns with your financial goals.

A - Assess and Adapt Budgeting Skills

Now, let's tackle the backbone of financial success—budgeting. In this segment, you'll be equipped with practical budgeting techniques to track your income and expenses effectively. We emphasize the importance of regular reviews and adjustments to ensure your financial goals are not just set but also achieved. Consider this your personalized financial GPS, helping you navigate the unsuspecting swerves of budgeting with confidence.

N - Navigate Borrowing and Debt

Borrowing money and accumulating debt can be treacherous waters, but fear not—this section is your compass. We'll educate you on the implications of borrowing, emphasizing responsible practices and strategies to avoid debt traps. By the end, you'll be equipped with the knowledge to navigate the borrowing landscape, making informed decisions that safeguard your financial future.

C - Cultivate a Savings Mindset

Saving money is more than just a habit; it's a mindset. In this chapter, we'll delve into the value of saving regularly and setting financial goals. Concepts like emergency funds, retirement savings, and the power of compound interest will become your allies. Consider this your initiation into the world of financial cultivation, where the seeds of your savings mindset are sown, ready to blossom into a prosperous financial future.

E - Empowerment through Action

Finally, we arrive at empowerment through action—the culmination of your journey. This section encourages you to take charge of your financial future by applying the knowledge and skills gained throughout the blueprint. We'll guide you to seek opportunities to earn, save, invest, and make informed financial decisions. This is not just about reading texts; it's about empowering you to take tangible steps toward financial independence.

Imagine a world where every dollar feels like it's slipping through your fingers, where financial confusion reigns, and where the road to financial independence seems like an insurmountable maze. Before the secrets within *Money Skills for Teen Blueprint* were uncovered, this world was a reality for many teenagers. In those days, financial concepts were like a foreign language, spoken fluently only by those with access to specialized knowledge. Budgeting wasn't a skill; it was a guessing game, and saving money felt like trying to catch a handful of sand in the wind. Teenagers juggled their allowances with uncertainty, often ending up in a cycle of impulsive spending and regret. It was an accepted norm to see a typical teenager navigate the complexities of adolescence, leaving behind a trail of unfulfilled desires. Budgeting was a vague notion, and saving for future goals felt like an unattainable dream. Financial independence seemed reserved for adults with their intricate knowledge of investments and savings.

Fast forward to a different scenario—a world painted by the transformative power of *Money Skills for Teen Blueprint*. In this reality, teenagers now easily grasp financial concepts with ease. The once obscure language of finance has become crystal clear, tailored explicitly to the unique needs of adolescents. Imagine flipping through these pages and finding the keys to unlocking the mysteries of money, with explanations so clear and concise that even the most complex concepts feel like second nature.

This book doesn't just promise; it delivers practical strategies and actionable tips that revolutionize the way teenagers manage their allowances—confidently navigating a well-structured budget, each expense planned with precision, discretionary funds allocated wisely, and financial decisions that aren't sources of stress but stepping stones toward a future of stability and prosperity. The guesswork is replaced by a systematic approach, turning financial chaos into a well-orchestrated symphony of financial management.

As you embark on this transformative journey through the F.I.N.A.N.C.E. Blueprint, remember that every chapter is crafted with your unique needs in mind. Your financial independence is not a distant goal; it's a series of practical steps, and this blueprint is your roadmap. Let's navigate these steps together, turning financial aspirations into a reality, one informed decision at a time!

ONE

Foundation Building

"Do you know that 75% of American teens lack confidence in their knowledge of personal finance?" (Turner, 2023). Startling stat, yeah? "Am I in this bracket?" "I hope I'm not in this bracket?" should be questions popping into your head right now. Well, it doesn't matter how many questions pop into your mind because of that stat. The important questions you should ask yourself are, "Do I have a comprehensive understanding of financial basics?" "Have I developed a sense of financial responsibility?" "Do I have a grasp of essential financial concepts?" "Have I made friends with responsible money management habits and cultivated a mindset conducive to achieving significant financial goals?" These questions are the basics of financial literacy —the magic booster of your confidence in personal finance. So, what are we saying? Your level of confidence in your personal finances starts with your level of financial literacy.

Now, get your engines fired up and get ready to move! As we cruise through this chapter, we'll get familiar with major ideas that form the foundations for building solid personal finances. Ready?

Understanding Financial Independence

Hey, teens, let's talk financial independence. Financial independence is like having a financial superhero moment. It's simply achieving the superhero level of adulthood. It's all about having the ability to make your own money picks and control what happens to your finances. Financial freedom means earning, saving, and spending money comfortably.

It's about having the freedom and resources to live your dream lifestyle without relying on others for money or asking for more assistance. Consider this: You cover your basic needs, such as housing and food, reward yourself with fun items, and still plan for your future with regard to finances. It's having the choice to choose how you spend your hard-earned bucks.

Here's an example: You get your first job and make some good money. Financial freedom begins when you can buy a concert ticket or save up for a big purchase without having to ask for additional money. It's about being able to cater and having that great awareness of control over your money.

Let's imagine you're getting ready for college and dreaming of freedom and excitement. Financial independence is the golden passport to making your desires a reality. Financial freedom covers more than simply textbooks and ramen noodles. You're also getting concert tickets, trying new hobbies, and saving for big adventures. There's no need to bother your parents for every cent; you're the master of your money ship. Your friends want to take a road trip over their break. Bam! Financial independence sets in. You have the funds to say, "Road trip?" "Let's roll!" No need to worry about scraping pennies together or waiting for a giveaway. That's the magic of financial independence—it's your passport to a world of possibilities, where you call the shots and turn your dreams into reality. You're the captain of your ship. No one pulls your strings. You decide how to live your best life without stressing about the next paycheck. It's your world, and you're the boss.

Basics of Financial Independence

Hey, future financial whizzes! Let's play around with the ABCs of personal finance. Let's talk about **income, expenses,** and **savings** —the trio that shapes your money journey. Imagine your **income** as the cash flowing into your wallet—it's not just about how much, but where it comes from. Allowances, part-time jobs, and gifts are like the three musketeers of income for teens—all different sources making your wallet go "cha-ching."

- **Allowances**: Your regular cash infusion. It's the money you get on a schedule—a bit like a paycheck for being awesome. Knowing how to budget helps you plan for your week, avoid impulse buys, and maybe even save a little.
- **Part-Time Jobs**: This is where you kick it up a notch. Whether it's babysitting, dog walking, or flipping burgers, part-time jobs bring in extra dough. They teach responsibility and time management, and hey, they look great on a resume, too!
- **Gifts**: Be it birthdays, holidays, or "just because," gifts are like little financial surprises. While they're not a regular thing, they're worth considering in your financial game plan. Maybe you'll stash some away for a big goal or treat yourself wisely. This idea should help you: when birthdays and holidays roll around and you receive some extra dough, it's like a surprise bonus, teaching you that unexpected windfalls can happen, too.

Now, let's sprinkle in a scenario or two to make it real. Imagine getting a generous birthday gift—instead of splurging on the latest gadget, think about saving a chunk. Over time, those savings can grow into something awesome, like a weekend getaway with friends or investing in something you're passionate about.

Remember, understanding income sources sets the stage for managing your money ninja-style. So, grab your financial toolkit, and let's build that solid foundation together!

Next up, **expenses**. You can call them stealthy villains. These are the cool things you spend your money on—like gaming gear, that epic online game subscription, hanging out with friends, or grabbing a snack. Imagine your money as a team, and expenses are the players. You want a balanced squad to keep the game going smoothly. But here's the plot twist: not all money should join the spending party. Enter **savings**—the MVP of financial stability. It's like setting aside a portion of your income for future adventures, big goals, or unexpected plot twists. Saving is your superhero move for financial independence!

Now, let's paint a picture. Imagine you get a weekly allowance of $25. That's your income. You spend $10 on snacks, $5 on a cool game, and save the remaining $10. You just created a winning strategy: balancing expenses and saving for future quests.

Importance and Techniques for Tracking Expenses to Understand Spending Habits

Now, let's talk about the spending side of the coin—tracking expenses. Think of it as your financial detective work, helping you understand where your money goes and how to make it work smarter for you. Tracking expenses is like having a backstage pass to your financial show. It lets you see where your hard-earned cash is taking center stage and where it might be sneakily slipping away. Knowing your spending habits helps you gain the power to make informed decisions, plug money leaks, and get more bang for your buck.

Some Expense Tracking Techniques

- **Keep a Spending Diary**: Jot down every purchase, no matter how small. It's like a financial diary, and you'll be surprised at the patterns you uncover.
- **Budgeting Apps**: Embrace the tech side! There are cool apps out there that can categorize your spending, giving you a visual breakdown of where your money's hanging out.
- **Envelopes or Jars**: Old-school but effective. Label envelopes or jars with categories like school supplies, entertainment, or snacks. Put a set amount in each at the start of the month, and when it's empty, that's it—no more spending in that category.

Now, Let's Bring in Some Relatable Examples

Imagine it's back-to-school season, and you've got some extra cash from your part-time gig. Instead of randomly grabbing supplies, make a list of what you need. Track prices, compare deals, and stick to your budget. This way, you'll have everything you need without burning a hole in your wallet. Or, let's say you love going to the movies with friends. Create an entertainment budget— decide how much you can afford to spend on movies, snacks, and maybe even a post-movie treat. By keeping tabs on these expenses, you ensure that movie nights are fun without turning your budget into a horror show. Be sure that tracking expenses isn't about restricting yourself; it's about making informed choices that align with your goals.

The Role of Financial Institutions in Managing Money

Alright, money maestros, buckle up because we're diving into the world of financial institutions—your money's trusty sidekicks in managing the financial adventure.

Role of Financial Institutions

- **Safe Haven for Savings:** Think of banks as your money's bodyguard. When you stash your cash in a savings account, it's not just hanging out under your mattress. It's in a secure place, and you might even earn a little extra in interest. Let's make you understand better. Imagine you've been diligently saving a portion of your allowance in a piggy bank. Cool, right? But what if your little brother thinks it's a treasure chest and "borrows" some coins? Enter a savings account at a bank—your money is safe, it grows a bit, and your little brother can't sneak a peek.

- **Payment Partners**: Ever use a debit card for that late-night pizza delivery? That's the magic of financial institutions. They provide tools like debit cards, checks, and online banking, making transactions a breeze. You score a part-time job and receive your first paycheck; instead of dealing with wads of cash, you opt for a digital wallet linked to your bank account. Now, with a few taps on your phone, you can pay for movie tickets or split the bill with friends without worrying about losing cash.

- **Borrowing Buddies**: When big dreams need a little financial boost, enter loans. Financial institutions can lend you money for things like education or a car. Dreaming of a shiny new laptop for school? Financial institutions can help by offering a loan. But it's crucial to understand the terms before diving in. Here's the catch—you need to understand the interest rates and repayment terms. It's like borrowing a friend's game console—awesome, but you need to give it back on time!

Financial institutions are like wise mentors in your financial journey. They offer tools, protection, and opportunities. So, embrace the power of banking, my financial apprentices, and let these institutions be your guides to money mastery!

Developing Financial Responsibility

Now, let's chat about two unsung heroes in the financial superhero lineup: accountability and integrity. Picture them as the key holders of financial responsibility, ensuring a solid fortress for your financial goals.

Importance of Accountability and Integrity in Financial Matters

- **Accountability**: This is your commitment to owning up to your financial choices. It's about recognizing that every decision, big or small, shapes your financial path. Whether it's a big purchase or a tiny treat, being accountable means understanding the impact of your decisions and taking responsibility for them. Own your money moves!
- **Integrity**: Think of integrity as your financial moral compass. It's about making honest, ethical choices, even when no one is watching—when it's just you and your wallet. It's about sticking to your budget and building trust with yourself and others.

Consequences of Overspending and Living beyond Means (Poor Money Management)

Now, to the not-so-fun part—the consequences of poor money management. Imagine your money as a limited resource, and overspending or living beyond your means is like playing with fire. Poor money management can result in the overspending trap, piled debts with interests, and other stressful situations. Let's learn from the experiences of some teens.

Dave, a teenager, constantly swiped his credit card without tracking expenses. Soon, he found himself facing a monstrous debt dragon. Interest piled up, and what started as a small flame turned into a financial inferno. The consequences? Dave had to work extra hours to slay the debt beast. Annie, a teen who loved the thrill of instant gratification, splurged on the latest gadgets and trendy clothes, moving wild with YOLO (You Only Live Once). However, when it came time for a school trip she really wanted to join, her overspending left her dreams deferred. The lesson? Balance short-term enjoyment with long-term goals. In another story, Jordan is a teen who constantly borrows money from friends but never pays it back. Soon, friends became wary, and the social circle shrank. Poor money management not only affects your wallet but can strain relationships, too.

Let's not even talk about Keren, who underestimated the importance of an emergency fund. When her phone unexpectedly died, she faced a stressful situation without the funds to fix it. Learning the hard way, Keren realized that being financially prepared reduces stress in unexpected moments.

The key takeaway? Accountability and integrity aren't just about avoiding trouble; they are your financial shields against the consequences we just saw. Be mindful of your choices, think about the long-term impact, and make decisions that align with your goals. It's like choosing the right path in a video game—each decision shapes your journey. So, embrace your inner financial hero, my friends, and let accountability and integrity be your trusted sidekicks!

Taking Ownership of Your Financial Decisions

Now, let's empower you to take the reins of your financial journey! It's time to be the CEO of your wallet and master the art of financial responsibility. Here are some practical tips to level up your money game:

1. **Develop a Budget**: Create your spending plan, also known as a budget. Jot down your income sources, whether it's allowances, part-time gigs, or gifts. Then, outline your fixed expenses (like phone bills) and flexible ones (like entertainment). Having a budget is like having a treasure map—it guides you to financial success.

2. **Explore Savings Options**: Explore different savings options. Whether it's a traditional savings account, a high-yield savings account, or even exploring investment opportunities, find what suits your financial goals. Imagine your savings as seeds—the more you plant, the bigger your financial garden grows.

3. **Practice Price Consciousness**: Become a savvy shopper! It's time to drop the unproven "big boy" and "big girl" egos. Compare prices, look for deals, and be mindful of discounts. It's like scoring bonus points in a game—every penny saved adds up. Price consciousness is your secret weapon against overspending.

4. **Open a Checking Account**: Take a step into the financial realm by opening a checking account. It's like your own financial hub where you manage your money. Learn to track transactions, understand fees, and master the art of responsible spending.

5. **Start Building Credit**: Think of credit as your financial reputation. Start building it early by using a credit card responsibly. Pay your bills on time, keep balances low, and

watch your credit score rise. Good credit is like having a golden ticket for future financial opportunities.

6. **Aim for Financial Freedom**: Picture this—financial freedom is like unlocking a new level in a game. It's the ability to make choices based on your desires, not just your financial obligations anymore. It's a balling stage! Embrace smart money moves today so you can enjoy the perks of financial freedom tomorrow.

Through this journey, don't be too hard on yourself because mistakes are part of the game, but the real challenge is learning from them. How do I earn from them? Take ownership of your financial decisions, adjust your strategy when needed, and keep leveling up. You've got this, young financial wizard!

Building a Strong Financial Mindset

Alright, young financial pioneers, let's wrap up this chapter with some powerful tools to fuel your journey toward financial success.

Fostering a Positive Attitude toward Money and Financial Success

1. **Embrace Learning**: Treat financial education like a game of discovery. The more you learn, the more powerful you become in navigating the money maze.

2. **Celebrate Progress**: Whether it's saving a little extra or sticking to your budget, celebrate your wins. It's like leveling up in a game—acknowledge your achievements, big or small.

3. **Visualize Success**: Imagine your financial goals coming to life. Visualization is your secret weapon to stay motivated. Picture your dream vacation, a car, or even financial independence—it keeps you focused on the prize.

Strategies for Realistic Goal Setting and Disciplined Planning

1. **Set SMART Goals**: Make your goals SMART—Specific, Measurable, Achievable, Relevant, and Time-bound. It's like giving your goals a GPS—a clear roadmap to success.
2. **Create a Game Plan**: Break down your goals into smaller, more achievable tasks. It's like completing levels in a game —each task brings you closer to the final victory.
3. **Stay Disciplined**: Discipline is your in-game power-up. Stick to your budget, consistently save, and make choices that align with your goals. It's the key to unlocking financial achievements. Consider these quotes:

Inspirational Quotes to Foster a Positive and Strong Financial Mindset

"Discipline is the bridge between goals and accomplishment."

Jim Rohn (Quotes, 2024)

"Don't give up what you want most for what you want now."

Zig Ziglar (Quotes, 2024)

Value of Patience, Perseverance, and Delayed Gratification

1. **Patience Pays Off**: Financial success is a marathon, not a sprint. Be patient with your progress, and remember, even the most successful players started at Level 1.
2. **Persevere Through Challenges**: Facing obstacles is part of the game. Learn from the challenges, adapt your strategy, and keep moving forward. Perseverance is your resilience skill in the financial adventure.

3. **Delayed Gratification**: Think of delayed gratification as saving up for an epic in-game reward. It means resisting the urge for instant pleasure to achieve greater long-term success.

Now, imagine the legendary financial players who conquered challenges—from Walt Disney, who was told he lacked creativity, to Steve Jobs, who was booted from his own company to Bill Gates, who watched his first company crumble like a pack of cards (E. Daily, 2014). They faced setbacks, but with patience, perseverance, and delayed gratification, they achieved financial greatness.

As we conclude this chapter, remember that you've built a strong foundation. The next level? Exploring investment opportunities! In Chapter 2, we'll delve into the exciting world of growing your money. Get ready to unlock the power of investments, my financial trailblazers!

Interactive Questions

1. What is the main role of financial institutions in managing money?

   a) Providing pizza discounts
   b) Safe haven for savings
   c) Organizing gaming tournaments
   d) Running a music streaming service

2. Which of the following is a consequence of poor money management mentioned in the chapter?

a) Winning a lottery
b) Building good credit
c) Financial hardship
d) Finding hidden treasure

3. What does developing a budget involve for teens?

a) Memorizing a list of numbers
b) Creating a spending plan
c) Learning to juggle
d) Writing a novel about money

4. Which trait acts as a financial compass in the chapter?

a) Forgetfulness
b) Accountability
c) Invisibility
d) Super speed

5. What is the significance of opening a checking account?

a) Learning to dance
b) Mastering card tricks
c) Managing money efficiently
d) Becoming a chef

6. Which SMART goal characteristic involves having a clear roadmap to success?

  a) Specific
  b) Achievable
  c) Relevant
  d) Time-bound

Fascinating Facts

1. **Money Artifacts**: Did you know the earliest form of money dates back to around 5000 B.C.? (Kusimba, 2017).
2. **Young Millionaires**: Some teenagers have become millionaires through entrepreneurial ventures. For instance, Moziah Bridges started a bow-tie business at the age of nine, becoming a young entrepreneur (CO 2024).
3. **Compound Interest Magic**: Albert Einstein referred to compound interest as the eighth wonder of the world. It has the power to make your money grow exponentially over time (Family 2023).
4. **Savings and Stars**: Astronauts can save money in space! NASA uses a currency system to manage astronaut expenses during missions (NASA, 2024).

TWO

Investment in Education

Hey there, savvy teens! Welcome to Chapter 2 of our journey toward financial freedom: "Investment in Education." Ever wondered how you can start building your wealth from a young age, setting the stage for a financially secure future? Well, today, we're diving into the exciting world of investment options, where your money can start working for you. Ready to unlock the secrets of stocks, bonds, and mutual funds? Let's roll!

Introduction to Investment Options

Let's get it this way. As the financial pro that you're becoming, you're planning for your holiday tour with your pals. I'm sure you would compare available transportation options to settle for one that suits your budget, comfort, time, or other preferences, right? So, just like there are different transportation options to your holiday tour destination, there are different routes to your financial dreamland! Let's look at them.

Stocks (Your Share of the Pie)

Assume you own a slice from your favorite pizza shop. That's like owning shares! When you buy shares, you become a part-owner of the company. Stocks, like the carnival ride of the financial world, can rise and fall. What's the goal? Find the next big thing and see your investment grow!

Let's consider Warren Buffett, a stock market sage whom we can nickname the Oracle of Omaha. He's like the Yoda of financial investing. Buffett made his money mostly by investing in stocks. His company, Berkshire Hathaway, owns shares (stock) in well-known companies, including Coca-Cola and Apple. Warren's strategy? Long-term thinking. He patiently holds onto his investments, allowing them to flourish like healthy plants.

> **Takeaway**: When tackled with a calm and patient perspective, stocks can produce significant long-term profits. Why don't you start observing the news about daily stock market movements to pick your interest?

> **Scenario Time**: Assume you purchased shares in a technology company. If they develop the next must-have gadget, your stock might skyrocket! However, remember that the market can be unpredictable, so be prepared. You invest in a high-risk stock. It may surge, making you a financial superstar, or decline, leaving you with fewer pizza slices. It's all about discovering your comfort zone.

Bonds (The Loan Game)

Have you ever lent funds to a friend, promising that they would repay you with interest? Bonds are like that. When you purchase a bond, you lend money to a business or the government. In return, there is a pledge to repay you with interest. Bonds are like the steady Eddy of investments, offering a more predictable outcome than stocks.

Let us meet Ray Dalio, the bond genius. He started Bridgewater Associates, one of the world's largest hedge funds. Dalio is well-known for his broad investment knowledge, which frequently involves the use of bonds to navigate market cycles. His knowledge of economic cycles and bond markets enabled him to predict and successfully manage the 2008 financial crisis.

Takeaway: Bonds can provide stability and serve as an escape route during economic downturns.

Scenario Time: You invest in government bonds. They're like the slow and steady turtle in the investment race. Regular interest payments keep rolling in, helping you build your wealth over time.

Mutual Funds (Teamwork Makes the Dream Work)

Visualize an all-you-can-eat dinner where everyone contributes their best cuisine. Mutual funds function similarly but with money. When you invest in a mutual fund, you are sharing your money with others to purchase a variety of stocks, bonds, and occasionally other assets. Collaboration for financial success!

It's Peter Lynch time! We can call him the Mutual Fund Maestro. Peter Lynch, a famous fund manager, guided Fidelity's Magellan Fund to amazing success. Lynch believes in the value of analyzing and understanding the companies in which you invest. His approach is to choose stocks with high growth future potential. This has resulted in the Magellan Fund's remarkable performance during his tenure.

Takeaway: Mutual funds, when managed by a trained professional, can be a diverse platform for stable economic growth.

Scenario Time: You put your money into a tech-focused mutual fund. If one company has a bad day, it won't splash mud on your entire investment. Team efforts—that's it!

The Risks and Rewards of Investing

Let's now discuss the rollercoaster ride of risks and rewards. Investing isn't all about rainbows and unicorns. Rather, it's like a rollercoaster with ups and downs. Stocks can both rise and fall. Bonds provide stability, but their rewards can be moderate. If you remember, mutual funds are a combination of everything, making them a balanced but not risk-free option. This is why diversifying your investments across multiple instruments is important.

Let's study! John Bogle is a Vanguard Index Pioneer. John Bogle was a pioneer in promoting index investing. He started Vanguard Group, focusing on low-cost index funds that monitor the market. Given that index funds provide a simple and cost-effective strategy to acquire exposure to the overall market while minimizing risks, Bogle believed in the simplicity of investing in the entire market rather than attempting to outsmart it. His view of investing and the introduction of the first index fund changed the way many people invest.

Nevertheless, with all that's been discussed, if you aim to succeed financially in business or investing, you have to take risks. You must embrace this reality. So, take some level of risk and accept those risks. Not taking any risks at all is the riskiest path to take.

I'm sure you know Elon Musk, a risk-taking entrepreneur. While not a regular investor, Elon Musk is worth mentioning. Musk, the genius behind Tesla and SpaceX, took chances that paid off handsomely. Investing in his businesses became like investing in a high-risk, high-reward stock. Musk's success demonstrates the potential profits from investing in innovative, forward-thinking enterprises.

Successful Investing: Importance and Strategies for Diversification in Investment Portfolios

Okay, you've got the basics. Now, let's talk about strategy. Investing is like playing chess—you need a plan. Diversification is key; don't put all your eggs (or money) in one basket. Regularly check in on your investments, but avoid emotionally influenced reactions to market moves. Remember, the tortoise often beats the hare in the investment race. You spread your investments across stocks, bonds, and mutual funds. It's like having a balanced diet for your financial health—not one food group takes all the medals.

Consider the thrilling stories of these investment-savvy teens in America.

At just eight years old, Jaydyn Carr started his investment journey by buying shares of GameStop in 2019. His interest in the stock market grew, and he continued to invest in various stocks, gaining attention for his financial intelligence. Jaydyn's story shows the potential young minds have if they can understand investment concepts early.

Sophia Castiblanco, a seventeen-year-old investor with returns exceeding six figures, purchased her first car—a Tesla. At fourteen, she began producing lifestyle content like self-care tutorials, which earned her TikTok brand deals and YouTube ad revenue. Castiblanco invested in Vanguard and Berkshire Hathaway index funds to start building long-term wealth.

Here's what Sophia Castiblanco says about investing:

"There is no minimum age to start investing. Investing in index funds diversifies your risk and gives you a more balanced portfolio. As for purchasing stocks? It's a long-term game. You're investing in your future. Remember to be patient. Let your investments grow over time."

(Coblentz, 2024)

Phew! We covered a lot today, and you've earned your virtual investment badge. Stocks, bonds, mutual funds—they're like the superheroes of your financial journey. Embrace the risks, relish the rewards, and always stay curious. As you embark on your investment adventure, remember this: knowledge is power, and you're now armed with the secrets of financial growth.

Understanding Banking Services

Types of Bank Accounts, Specs, and Benefits

Hey, future financial wizards! Today, we're diving into the world of banking, your money's home base. Let's talk about the VIPs of banking services: checking accounts, savings accounts, and certificates of deposit (CDs).

1. Checking Accounts (Your Everyday Buddy)

Imagine your checking account as your backstage pass to money management. It's the account for everyday transactions—buying that cool gadget, grabbing a snack, or ordering online. With a debit card and checks, it's like having a magic wand for your daily spending. Just watch out for any sneaky fees—some banks charge if you go below a certain balance.

Tip: Look for a checking account with low fees and easy access to ATMs—convenience is key!

2. Savings Accounts (The Treasure Chest)

Now, let's talk about savings accounts—your treasure chest for goals, big or small. They offer a safe space to stash away money for emergencies or that dream vacation. The bonus? You earn interest on the money you keep in there. It's like your money-making little money babies.

Tip: Hunt for a savings account with a sweet interest rate and no or low fees—your money should work for you!

3. Certificates of Deposit (CDs) (The Time-Traveling Safe)

Ever wish you could time-travel to a future with more money? That's what a Certificate of Deposit (CD) does. You lock in your money for a set period, and in return, the bank pays you back with interest—kinda like a time-traveling safe that grows your money. Keep in mind, though, that it's not as flexible as the other accounts.

Tip: If you're sure you won't need the money soon, a CD can be a nifty way to watch your savings grow.

Practical Tips for Choosing Your Banking BFF: Tips and Tricks

Now, how do you pick the right bank and account for you? It's like finding your perfect match. Consider these practical tips:

1. **Fees, Fees, Fees**: Watch out for sneaky fees—monthly maintenance, ATM, or overdraft fees can add up. Look for accounts with minimal or no fees.
2. **Interest Rates**: Higher interest rates on savings accounts and CDs mean more money for you. Aim for the best rates to supercharge your savings.
3. **Accessibility**: Can you easily access your money when you need it? Check for a bank with a good online platform and ATMs nearby.

4. **Perks and Rewards**: Some banks offer cool perks—like cashback rewards or discounts. It's like getting a bonus for choosing them.

5. **Customer Service**: A friendly, helpful customer service team can make your banking experience a breeze. Don't settle for less!

Don't let this slip off you; your choice of bank and account should align with your goals. Whether you're a spending pro, a saving superhero, or a time-traveling money wizard, the right banking buddy is out there for you. Happy banking, future financial gurus!

Exploring the World of Stocks, Bonds, and Funds (SBF)

Alright, young financial adventurers, buckle up because we're taking a further ride into the financial playground of stocks, bonds, and funds. Let's break it down without the capes and masks.

SBF (Not Sam Bankman-Fried 😂)

1. **Stocks** (Ownership in Companies)

First off, stocks. We discussed this earlier, right? Well, let's do this again in another way. When you own a stock, you own a tiny piece of a company. It's like sitting in a meeting with the owners of the company to contribute your points—having a say in their decisions. Companies sell stocks to raise money for things like growing their business or launching new products. As a stockholder, you may also get a slice of their profits in the form of dividends.

Tip: Diversify your superhero team—don't put all your money on one hero. Spread the risk!

2. Bonds (Loaning Money to Governments and Companies)

Now, bonds. In our last gist on this, we agreed to think of bonds as loans you give to governments or companies, right? Right! So, when you buy a bond, you're lending them money, and, in return, they promise to pay you back with interest. It's a bit like being a helpful friend who gets a little extra for the favor.

Tip: Think of bonds as your financial sidekick, balancing out the excitement of stocks with a steady income stream.

3. Funds (Teamwork Makes the Dream Work)

Next up, funds. These are like the Avengers of the financial world. Instead of buying individual stocks or bonds, you pool your money with others into a fund. This fund then invests in a mix of stocks, bonds, and sometimes other assets. Teamwork for financial growth!

Tip: Funds are a great way to win an arcade battle without having to pick individual heroes to fight for you.

Risk and Reward (The Investment Dance)

Now, let's talk about risk and reward—the yin and yang of investing. Stocks are like thrill-seekers; their value can swing up and down dramatically. Higher risk, yes, but potentially higher reward. It's like swinging between skyscrapers—exhilarating but not without its heart-stopping moments. Bonds, on the other hand, are more like the steady planners. They offer stability but with more modest returns. In other words, while they might not bring the same adrenaline rush as stocks, they offer stability and regular income. The key? Finding the right balance that fits your comfort level. Understand your risk tolerance—how much excitement (or stress) can you handle?

Let's take a sample. If you invest in a high-risk stock, the excitement comes from the potential for big gains, but there's also a chance of significant losses. On the flip side, bonds may not have the same adrenaline rush, but they provide a smoother, less bumpy ride.

Understanding the Roles of Stocks, Bonds, and Funds – Financing Companies and Governments

These financial instruments play a crucial role in the big picture. Companies use stocks and bonds to raise funds for growth and development. Governments use bonds to finance projects like building infrastructure or funding public services. So, when you invest in stocks or bonds, you're essentially contributing to the progress of companies and governments.

In a nutshell, stocks, bonds, and funds are like the gears in the financial machinery, working together to drive economic growth. Understanding their functions and the delicate dance of risk and reward is your passport to navigating the exciting world of investing. Ready to make some informed financial moves? Let's do this!

Mastering Investment Strategies

Hey, future financial maestros! Now that we've explored the realm of stocks and bonds, it's time to talk strategy—the secret sauce to growing your wealth. Let's uncover two cool strategies: Dollar-Cost Averaging and Value Investing.

1. Dollar-Cost Averaging (The Consistent Saver)

Picture this: You decide to invest a fixed amount regularly, regardless of market ups and downs. That's dollar-cost averaging! It's like regularly buying your favorite snacks on a fixed day within the week, whether the price is high or low. Over time, this strategy can smooth out the bumps in market price changes.

Let's assume you invest $50 in a stock every month. In some months, the price is high, and in some months, it's low. By consistently investing, you end up buying more shares when prices are low and fewer when prices are high, averaging your overall cost.

2. **Value Investing** (The Bargain Hunter)

Ever found a great deal on something you love? Value investing is a bit like that. You look for stocks that seem undervalued compared to their true worth. It's about finding hidden gems in the stock market, like discovering a high-end gadget on sale at a bargain price.

Let's assume you do your research and find a company with strong fundamentals, but its stock price is temporarily low due to market fluctuations. You invest, anticipating that the market will recognize the company's value over time, leading to potential gains. That's value investing!

Learning from the Masters: The Buffetts and the Bubbles

Now, let's peek into history. Warren Buffett, a legendary investor, swears by value investing. His patient approach turned Berkshire Hathaway into a financial juggernaut. On the flip side, there's the infamous dot-com bubble in the late '90s. Investors went wild for tech stocks, only to see many crash and burn. Lesson learned: Avoid jumping on bandwagons without doing your homework.

So, here's the deal—investing isn't just about throwing money at stocks and hoping for the best. It's a thoughtful journey. Dollar-cost averaging keeps you disciplined, and value investing sharpens your bargain-hunting skills. Remember, the market can be a thrilling rollercoaster, but with the right strategies, you can enjoy the ride.

Ready for the next chapter? We're stepping into the world of "Nurturing Smart Spending Habits." Your newfound knowledge is your ticket to mastering not just investing but also making savvy choices with your hard-earned money. Get ready to level up your financial game!

Interactive Questions

Now, let's flex our mental muscles with these questions.

1. What is the definition of a stock?

    a) A loan provided to a corporation
    b) A share of ownership in a company
    c) A type of bond issued by the government
    d) A savings account offered by banks

2. What is the primary purpose of bonds?

    a) To provide ownership rights in a company
    b) To generate dividends for shareholders
    c) To offer high returns with low risk
    d) To represent a loan to a corporation or government

Fascinating Facts

1. **The Barbie Doll IPO**: When the Barbie doll was first launched in 1959, it was an instant success. If you had invested $1,000 in Mattel's first public offering (IPO), the business that created Barbie, it would now be worth

millions. Barbie is not just a fashion icon but also a successful investment!

2. **Lunar Real Estate:** In 1997, Dennis Hope claimed ownership of the moon and other planetary bodies. He began selling plots of lunar real estate to investors. While this may seem absurd, over 6 million people have purchased a piece of the moon, making Hope a billionaire in the most unusual way.

THREE

Nurture Smart Spending Habits

Have you ever wondered how you can make your money work smarter for you? This chapter will empower you with practical strategies to nurture smart spending habits and achieve your financial goals.

Differentiating Needs from Wants

Alright, let's dive into the world of needs and wants. Picture this: You've got a wad of cash, and there's a world of possibilities. Now, needs are the essentials—the things you can't live without. Wants? Well, they're the cool extras that make life more enjoyable but aren't crucial for survival.

Needs are like your survival toolkit. Think food, a roof over your head, and clothes on your back. These are nonnegotiable. You can't live on air, and your phone won't shield you from the rain. These are the must-haves for basic survival and functioning.

Wants, on the other hand, are the sprinkles on your ice cream. Imagine a new video game, trendy sneakers, or that sleek gadget everyone's talking about. While these things can add excitement to life, they aren't vital. You won't starve without the latest gaming console, trust me.

Distinguishing between Essential Expenses (Needs) and Discretionary Spending (Wants)

Now, let's talk about practical scenarios. Imagine you're at the mall, eyeing a fantastic pair of sneakers. Are your current shoes still kicking? If yes, that desire might fall into the "want" category. If your current shoes are hanging by a thread, it could lean toward a "need." See how that works?

Here's another one—your phone is on the fritz, and you're tempted by the allure of the latest model. Ask yourself—is your current phone still doing its job, or is it more like a relic from ancient times? If it's still getting the job done, the new one might just be a want.

In a nutshell, needs keep you alive and functional; wants add a dash of fun. Before you hit that checkout button or swipe your card, ask yourself, "Is this a must-have for survival or just a nice-to-have for fun?" It's the golden question that can guide your spending decisions and lead you down the road of smart, conscious consumption.

Being a savvy spender isn't about being a penny-pincher; it's about making choices that align with your goals and values. So, the next time you're faced with a spending dilemma, give it some thought: needs first, sprinkle wants on top. Your wallet—and future self—will thank you for it.

Strategies for Prioritizing Needs While Minimizing Unnecessary Expenses

Alright, let's talk about mastering the art of prioritizing needs and keeping those unnecessary expenses in check. Imagine your money is like a team—each dollar has a role, and you're the coach deciding where they play. Or imagine you're torn between saving up for a school trip or splurging on the latest tech gadget. The trip might be a need if it's part of your education or personal growth, while the gadget is more of a want. Prioritizing needs over wants means putting the essentials and significant goals first—it's like creating a roadmap for your money. Check out these strategies below:

1. Know Your Essentials

Start by identifying your team's MVPs—the Most Valuable Purchases. These are your needs: food, shelter, clothing, and things directly tied to your education. Make a list, and let these essentials take the starting positions.

2. Set Goals

Imagine your money as players on the field. What's the endgame? Is it saving up for a cool gadget or contributing to a meaningful goal like a school trip? Clearly define your financial goals. When you know where you're headed, it's easier to make choices that score points for your future self.

3. Budget Like a Pro

Create a game plan for your money with a budget. Allocate specific amounts to your needs and goals. This isn't about restricting yourself; it's about making sure your dollars are playing the right positions. Budgeting helps you see where your money is going and keeps you in control of the game.

4. Delay Gratification

Sometimes, that tempting "want" is waving at you from the sidelines. Take a pause. Ask yourself if it's the right time. Can it wait until your financial team is in a stronger position? Delaying gratification is like saving your energy for the crucial moments in the game.

5. Make Informed Choices

Before making a purchase, do your homework. Compare prices, read reviews, and explore alternatives. Being an informed shopper ensures you're getting the best value for your money, making every play count.

6. Avoid Impulse Moves

Impulse buys are like surprise moves on the field—exciting but not always the best strategy. When faced with a shiny new "want," take a moment. Does it align with your goals? Is it a smart play or just a fleeting excitement? Avoiding impulsive spending keeps your financial game plan on track.

7. Embrace Thriftiness

Being thrifty isn't about sacrificing fun; it's about finding smart alternatives. Thrift stores, discounts, and sales can be your secret weapons. Why pay full price when you can get the same value for less? Being thrifty allows you to stretch your financial muscles without breaking the bank.

8. Review and Adjust

Remember, even the best coaches tweak their strategies. Regularly review your budget and spending habits. Are you staying on track with your goals? Adjust as needed to ensure your financial team is always at peak performance.

In the game of smart spending, the goal isn't to avoid spending altogether—it's about making every dollar count. By prioritizing needs and minimizing unnecessary expenses, you're not just managing money; you're becoming the coach of your financial team, steering it toward success. So, gear up, set your goals, and let's play the game of financial success—you've got this!

Setting Financial Priorities

Allocating Resources to Financial Priorities Wisely

Alright, let's talk about setting your financial priorities, which is a bit like crafting your game strategy. Imagine your money as players on the field—each with a unique role. Here's how to decide who gets the ball and when:

1. Define Your Goals

Start by envisioning your dream game—what do you want to achieve with your money? Is it scoring points for a new gaming console or making a game-changing move toward a meaningful goal like saving for a school trip? Clearly define your financial goals; they're your playbook.

2. Prioritize Based on Values

Think about what truly matters to you. Your values are like the rules of your game—they guide your decisions. If education is a top priority, allocating funds toward books or educational resources makes sense. If connecting with friends is vital, saving for social events may take the lead.

3. Short Term vs. Long Term

Here's where the game gets interesting: Short-term desires are like quick passes—thrilling but fleeting. Long-term goals are more strategic, like setting up the perfect play for future success. Balance is key. Allocate resources wisely, ensuring you're not sacrificing long-term touchdowns for short-term gains.

4. Allocate Resources Wisely

Now, it's time to draw up your plays. In your budget, assign specific amounts to different goals and necessities. A budget isn't about restrictions; it's your personalized playbook, ensuring every dollar has a role in achieving your financial game plan.

5. Learn to Pivot

Life throws unexpected curveballs, and your financial game plan may need adjustments. Be flexible and ready to pivot when necessary. It's like adapting your strategy mid-game to ensure you're always moving toward your goals, even if the path changes.

6. Save for the Future

Long-term goals are the championship matches of your financial game. Allocate a portion of your resources to savings, creating a safety net for the future. Whether it's for higher education, a dream trip, or an entrepreneurial venture, saving ensures you're ready for the big leagues.

7. Avoid Distractions

Just like in a game, there are distractions in the financial field. The latest trends, impulse buys—they're like opponents trying to throw you off course. Stay focused on your priorities. Evaluate each financial move against your goals to avoid getting sidelined.

8. Celebrate Victories

Every touchdown, big or small, deserves celebration. When you achieve a financial goal, acknowledge your success. It's not just about the final score; it's about recognizing your progress and staying motivated for the next play.

Dear teenager, you've got the power to make every move count!

Identifying Financial Priorities and Aligning with Values

Imagine that you're passionate about environmental issues. Your financial priority might be to support eco-friendly initiatives or invest in sustainable products. When you allocate a portion of your resources to eco-friendly choices, you're not just spending money—you're investing in something that aligns with your values.

Finley Lewis

Tap motivation from a fifteen-year-old investor, Finley Lewis, who grew $300 to over $5,000 over just three years and then wrote a book to help teenagers grow their wealth. He combined the valuable lessons that he learned growing up in a financially conscious household and his priorities as an investor to publish what is essentially a rulebook for teens (Scott-Briggs, 2023). Read what Finley Lewis says,

> *"You're never too young to learn about money ... In fact, the younger you are, the better."*

> Lewis, 2023

Greta Thunberg

You can also draw inspiration from Greta Thunberg, who, from her teenage years, identified climate change as a priority. Greta aligned her actions with her values by reducing her carbon footprint and advocating for environmental change. At fifteen, Thunberg held the first "School Strike for Climate" outside the

Swedish parliament. In so doing, she turned her passion into a powerful force for positive impact. Her values are webbed around being different and maintaining uniqueness. Here are her words:

"Being different is a gift, if I would've been like everyone else, I wouldn't have started this ..."

(BBC, 2023)

Today, Thunberg is one of the world's best-known climate change campaigners, traveling around the world addressing crowds at marches and protests. In 2019, she became the youngest-ever Time Person of the Year and has been nominated for the Nobel Peace Prize every year between 2019 and 2023. Thunberg's secret? She identified her financial priorities in advocacy for climate change, then aligned them with her values, and boom! Here she is today.

Balancing Short-Term Desires with Long-Term Objectives

Let's assume you dream of attending a top-notch university. While friends might be splurging on the latest gadgets, you choose to allocate a portion of your part-time job income to a college fund. This short-term sacrifice of immediate pleasures is a strategic move to secure a better future, allowing you to pursue higher education without overwhelming student loans.

You can take a leaf from Mark Zuckerberg, the co-founder of Facebook, who set clear financial goals early in life. While studying at Harvard, he focused on creating a social networking platform that eventually became Facebook. Facebook's early days were neither when the service had gone mainstream nor when it was popular only within the Harvard community. The early days were the times when Mark sacrificed immediate pleasures to pursue his long-term vision.

We can also consider Bethany Mota, a successful YouTuber and entrepreneur who started creating videos in her teens. She identified her passion for fashion and beauty and aligned her financial priorities with her values. By balancing short-term content creation with long-term goals, Bethany turned her hobby into a thriving career. What does Bethany's story teach? Your short-term desires may not be bad in themselves. But you should learn how to align them with long-term objectives. Your regular fashion videos on YouTube aren't bad in themselves. However, learn to be strategic about it and have a long-term objective for it.

Practicing Conscious Consumption

Alright, let's talk about practicing conscious consumption—a fancy term for being a smart, thoughtful shopper. It's like having a prompter that helps you make decisions that align with your goals. Ready? Let's dive in!

Strategies for Mindful Spending Habits

1. **Think before You Swipe**

Before reaching for your wallet, take a moment. Ask yourself: Do I really need this? How does it align with my goals? It's like giving your brain a little workout before your wallet does the heavy lifting. This pause can make a big difference in steering clear of regrettable purchases.

2. **Comparison Shopping**

Imagine you're on a quest for the perfect pair of sneakers. Don't settle for the first one that catches your eye. Explore different options, compare prices, and read reviews—it's like creating a shopping strategy. By doing this, you ensure you're getting the best deal and the most value for your hard-earned money.

3. The Waiting Game

For nonessential purchases, introduce a waiting period. It's like pressing pause on that desire and giving yourself time to think it over. If, after a bit of waiting, you still really want it and it aligns with your goals, then go for it. This strategy is your secret weapon against impulse buying.

4. Avoid Impulse Buying

Speaking of impulse buying, it's like the sneak attack of shopping. Avoid it by having a game plan. Stick to your shopping list, and if something catches your eye that wasn't on the list, give it the critical thinking test. Is it a want or a need? Does it align with your goals? If not, it can wait.

5. Budgeting for Fun

Yes, we're bringing budgeting back into the game. Allocate a portion of your budget for the fun stuff. It's like giving yourself permission to enjoy without feeling guilty. This way, you can indulge in your desires guilt-free while keeping your overall financial game plan intact.

6. Needs First, Wants Later

Remember our MVPs from earlier—needs and wants? Prioritize your needs and tackle them first. It's like getting the fundamentals right before diving into the extras. Once your essentials are covered, you can allocate some funds for those cool extras guilt-free.

7. Quality over Quantity

Imagine you're building a team of possessions. It's not about having the most players; it's about having the best players. Invest in quality items that last longer and align with your values. It's like building a dream team of possessions that serve you well over time.

8. Be a Smart Shopper

Finally, embrace the art of being a smart shopper. Hunt for deals, use discounts, and take advantage of sales. It's like unlocking bonus levels in the game of shopping. Being a savvy shopper ensures you get more bang for your buck.

So, there you have it—the playbook for practicing conscious consumption. By thinking critically, comparing options, waiting for nonessential purchases, and avoiding impulse buying, you're not just shopping; you're making choices that elevate your financial game. It's like turning every shopping trip into a victory for your wallet and your financial future. Game on!

Environmental and Social Impacts of Consumer Choices

Let's chat about the bigger picture, something that goes beyond our wallets – the ripple effect of our consumer choices- and how our choices as consumers can make a positive impact on the world around us. It's like leveling up in the game of responsible living. Ready? Let's dive in!

1. Environmental Impacts

Picture this: Every item you buy has a story, and that story often involves the environment. Responsible consumption is like being a hero for the planet. Ever heard of the three Rs—Reduce, Reuse, Recycle? It's like the golden rule of responsible consumption. Opt for eco-friendly products, choose items with minimal packaging, and recycle. It's the small choices that collectively make a big difference. For example, choosing a reusable water bottle over a disposable one reduces plastic waste and helps keep our oceans cleaner.

2. Social Impacts

Now, let's talk about the people behind the products. Your choices as a consumer can impact communities and workers around the world. Opting for fair-trade products ensures that the people involved in production receive fair wages and work in safe conditions. Explore brands with a conscience by supporting businesses. When you support companies that contribute to education, healthcare, or local projects, thus becoming agents of empowerment, you contribute to community well-being. Imagine your purchase as a vote—a vote for fair treatment and ethical practices.

Furthermore, think local! Buying from local businesses not only supports your community but also reduces the environmental impact of transporting goods over long distances. It's like putting money back into the neighborhood and helping local businesses thrive.

So, there you have it—the power-packed impact of responsible consumption. Every choice we make as consumers ripples beyond our shopping bags, influencing the planet, communities, and even the values we champion. It's like turning every purchase into a chance for a better world. Let's make our consumer choices count —not just for us but for Team Earth, Team Humanity, and Team Goodness! Game on!

Now that we've explored the broader impact of our choices, let's shift our focus to mastering budgeting skills—the essential playbook for effective financial management. In the next chapter,

"Assess and Adapt Budgeting Skills," we'll dive into practical strategies to manage your money effectively, setting the stage for achieving your financial goals. Think of it as the roadmap that turns your aspirations into reality. So, gear up and get ready to conquer the world of budgeting—your financial adventure awaits in Chapter 4!

Fascinating Facts

1. Did you know that by 2050, there could be more plastic in the ocean than fish? (Foundation, 2024).
2. In the world of sustainable fashion, pineapple leaves are stealing the show. Brands are turning pineapple waste into durable and stylish fabrics. Pineapple leather, also known as Piñatex, is a cruelty-free alternative that looks chic and supports sustainability (Matt. 2023).
3. Have you heard of the Tiny House Movement? Some folks are downsizing their living spaces, not just for simplicity but also to minimize their environmental footprint. Tiny houses use fewer resources and energy, showcasing a creative way to live sustainably (Andrew, 2023).

Financial Habits Quiz

Instructions: Answer the following questions honestly by selecting the option that best describes your current spending habits:

1. How often do you check your bank account balance?

    a) Daily
    b) Weekly
    c) Monthly
    d) Rarely or never

2. When you receive money (e.g., allowance, gifts), what do you usually do with it?

    a) Save a portion and spend the rest
    b) Spend it all immediately
    c) Save it all for a specific goal
    d) Not sure

3. How often do you create a budget for your expenses?

    a) Every month
    b) Occasionally
    c) Rarely
    d) Never

4. What percentage of your income do you typically save?

    a) More than 20%
    b) 10–20%
    c) Less than 10%
    d) I don't save any of my income

5. How often do you make impulse purchases?

    a) Rarely or never
    b) Occasionally
    c) Frequently
    d) Always

6. When deciding whether to buy something, what factors do you consider most?

    a) Price and utility
    b) Brand and popularity
    c) Peer pressure and trends
    d) Not sure

7. How often do you track your expenses?

    a) Daily
    b) Weekly
    c) Monthly
    d) Rarely or never

8. Do you have any long-term financial goals?

    a) Yes, and I'm actively working toward them
    b) Yes, but I haven't started working toward them yet
    c) No, I haven't thought about it
    d) Not sure

Scoring:

For each A response, give yourself 2 points.
For each B response, give yourself 1 point.

For each C response, give yourself 0 points.

For each D response, give yourself -1 point.

Interpretation:

Score 14–16: Congratulations! You have excellent financial habits.

Score 8–13: You're doing fairly well, but there's room for improvement.

Score 0–7: You may need to rethink some of your spending habits and consider making changes to improve your financial well-being.

Make a Difference with Your Review

UNLOCK THE POWER OF GENEROSITY

"Money can't buy happiness, but giving it away sure feels good!"

Inspired by Freddie Mercury

Did you know people who give without expecting anything in return tend to be happier and more successful? That's something I really believe in, and I want to share that secret with you!

So, I have a small but mighty favor to ask...

Would you be willing to help out someone you've never met, with no strings attached?

Who is this mystery person, you ask? Well, they're a lot like you once were: eager to learn, looking to make smart money moves, but unsure where to start.

Our goal is to make "Money Skills for Teens" a go-to resource for every young person out there. Everything we do is driven by this mission. But to reach everyone, we really need your help.

A lot of people decide whether to read a book based on its reviews. So here's my big ask on behalf of a Teen somewhere out there who needs a guiding hand:

Could you leave a review for this book?

It doesn't cost a dime and takes less than a minute, but your words could change another Teen's life forever. Your review might help:

- One more small business thrive in its community.

- One more entrepreneur support their family.
- One more employee find meaningful work.
- One more client transform their life.
- One more dream come true.

To spread those good vibes and truly make a difference, all you need to do is: **Leave a review.**

Just scan the QR code below to share your thoughts:

If the idea of helping out a faceless Teen warms your heart, then you're definitely my kind of person! Welcome to the club—you're one of us now.

I'm super excited to help you **Unlock Financial Independence EASIER** than you ever imagined. You're going to love the strategies I have in store for you in the upcoming chapters.

Thank you from the bottom of my heart. Let's get back to learning and fun!

- Your biggest fan, D. McClarence

PS - Fun fact: When you offer something valuable to someone else, it increases your own value to them. If you think this book can help another Teen, why not share it with them?

FOUR

Assess and Adapt Budgeting Skills

Have you ever struggled to stretch your allowance or part-time earnings until the next payday? I mean, when regular allowances inflow your accounts, you're excited, especially when there's some form of top-up from an extra side gig that'll buffer your balances. However, a couple of days into the month, your money seems to have developed wings and whim! Out they go—into thin air, and you can't wrap your head around what's happening. In the end, you borrow from friends or do more credit card swipes to meet up with expenses for the rest of the month while biting your fingers in the stands awaiting the next pay. Meanwhile, it's only the 15th of January.

If you've ever had this struggle, this chapter dives into essential budgeting skills to help you confidently navigate your finances.

Tracking Income and Expenses

Financial pros-in-the-making, your allowance, a part-time job, those birthday gifts, and even your usual website subscription are all players in your financial game. Tracking them is like keeping score or a bit like becoming the financial detective of your own life. Let's break it down.

The Importance of Accurately Tracking Sources of Income

Income isn't just that crisp bill you find in your pocket. It's the money flowing into your life. Moreover, it's not just about knowing how much it is but where it comes from, and the more you know about it, the better.

Imagine your income as the fuel for your financial adventure. It's not just about allowances—it's the money from part-time jobs, gifts, or any other sources. Accurately tracking your income is like knowing how much gas you have in the tank. It helps you plan your journey wisely. For example, if you're earning from a part-time job, keeping track ensures you don't underestimate your financial resources and can plan accordingly.

Tracking Expenses

Now, let's talk about expenses—the destinations on your financial map. They come in two flavors: fixed and variable. Fixed expenses are like the steady landmarks on your journey—rent, utilities, or your phone bill. They stay consistent. Variable expenses, on the other hand, are like pit stops—they can change. Think entertainment, dining out, or those occasional splurges. Given that expenses come in two flavors, you have to respect this reality and capture it in your budget.

Categorizing your expenses is like putting different destinations into zones on your map. Fixed expenses are in one zone, and variable expenses are in another. This helps you see where your money is going and plan your route accordingly.

Let's break it down with some scenarios.

Let's say your phone bill is due every month—that's a fixed expense. It's like a regular toll on your financial highway. Knowing it's coming allows you to budget for it, making sure you have the funds when it's time to pay up.

Now, imagine a movie night with friends—that's a variable expense. It's like a drift from your usual route. By categorizing it as a variable expense, you're aware that it might not happen every month, helping you plan for it when it does.

So, why all of this? Well, the idea behind tracking your income and categorizing your expenses is not about trying to make you joggle numbers to intensify your intellectual capacity, nor is it about placing overly high walls to restrict you. Rather, it's an attempt to make you understand your financial landscape. By doing this, you'll be like a skilled navigator, steering clear of financial potholes and ensuring a smoother journey toward your goals. Remember, your money is your adventure fund, and accurate tracking ensures you have the right map to explore the financial world confidently. Ready for the next step?

Tools and Techniques for Recording Transactions

Alright, soon-to-be budgeting models, let's talk about the tools and techniques that will turn you into financial wizards—the kind who navigate their money bags with ease. Ready to unlock the secrets of recording transactions? Let's dive in!

Budgeting Apps

Imagine having a sidekick that helps you keep track of every financial move you make. That's where budgeting apps swoop in to save the day! These nifty tools live in your phone, ready to assist you in recording income, categorizing expenses, and even creating visual reports of your financial landscape. Apps like Mint, PocketGuard, or YNAB (You Need A Budget) can be your digital sidekick, making the tracking process smoother than ever. Let's see why they're awesome:

Real-Time Updates: Most apps sync with your bank accounts, giving you real-time updates. It's like having a live feed of your financial world.

Category Magic: They automatically categorize your expenses, saving you the trouble of sorting through receipts. It's like having a magical assistant organizing your financial potion ingredients.

Visual Reports: Budgeting apps often provide colorful charts and graphs. It's like turning your financial data into a simple, captivating comic book—engaging and easy to understand.

Budgeting Worksheets

Now, let's talk about the old-school day savers—budgeting worksheets. These are like the trusty sidekicks that never go out of style. They come in various forms, whether you prefer a printable sheet or an Excel wizardry. These worksheets let you manually record your income and expenses, giving you a hands-on approach to mastering your financial universe.

Why They're Awesome

Hands-On Learning: Worksheets make you an active participant in your budgeting journey. It's like crafting your financial story with your own hands.

Customizable: You can tailor worksheets to suit your

preferences. It's like having a superhero costume that fits perfectly—uniquely yours.

Analog Connection: Some find joy in the tangible feel of writing things down. It's like connecting with the roots of budgeting—a timeless practice.

Tips for Using Tools

Choose Your Sidekicks: Always do what works for you. Pick the tool that resonates with you. Apps are dynamic, and worksheets offer a personal touch—it's all about finding your superhero companion.

Set Up Regular Check-Ins: Whether it's weekly or monthly, schedule regular check-ins with your budgeting tool. It's like giving your sidekick a debrief on your financial adventures.

Celebrate Progress: When you hit financial milestones, celebrate! It's like leveling up in the game of budgeting—acknowledgment keeps you motivated.

So, whether you're "team app" or "team worksheet," the key is to find a sidekick that empowers you on your budgeting journey. Ready to wield these financial tools like a true budgeting superhero? The adventure awaits, and you've got the power to conquer your financial universe! Onward to financial greatness!

Creating a Realistic Budget

Alright, budgeting champs, let's break down the steps to creating a budget that's as unique as you are. It's like crafting a passable route for your financial journey. Ready? Let's get started!

Steps to Creating a Realistic Budget

Step 1: Figure Out How Much You Make

The first move in your budgeting dance is figuring out your income. It's not just allowances—including part-time job earnings, gifts, or any other money flowing your way. This is your starting point—the cash you have to play with.

Step 2: Keep a Record of Your Expenses

Now, let's shine a light on your spending habits. Keep a record of every cent you spend, from your morning coffee to that occasional movie night. This snapshot gives you the real deal on where your money is going.

Step 3: Identify Where You're Spending

Time to dissect that spending list. Categorize your expenses into groups like rent, utilities, entertainment, and so on. This helps you see where your money is hanging out the most.

Step 4: Subtract the Total Spent on Necessities from Your Earnings

Now for the math magic. Subtract the total spent on necessities like rent and utilities from your earnings. What's left is your play money—the funds you have for nonessentials.

Step 5: Create Savings Goals

Goals are like your financial destinations. Want a cool gadget? Planning a trip? Set savings goals for them. It's like deciding where you want to go on your financial map.

Step 6: Decide How and How Much You Want to Save Each Budget Cycle

How much of your play money do you want to tuck away for those goals? Decide on a percentage or a fixed amount to save each budget cycle. It's like drafting your savings strategy.

Step 7: Start Using Your Budget and Stick to It

Now, it's showtime. Start using your budget like a playbook for your money. Stick to it as closely as you can—it's your guide to financial success.

Step 8: Check-In and Reevaluate If Needed

As you journey through the budgeting landscape, make pit stops to check-in. If things change—like getting a new job or having new expenses—reevaluate your budget. Flexibility keeps your financial chart accurate.

Scenarios

- Let's say your total earnings are $200, and your necessities cost $120. Subtracting that leaves you with $80 for nonessentials. You decide to save $50 for a future goal, leaving you with $30 to spend on fun stuff. Wise, isn't it?
- Let's see another. If your goal is to save for a phone upgrade, decide how much you want to save each budget cycle. Let's say $15. That's like putting away a small portion each time, making it manageable and achievable.

Creating a budget is like sculpting your financial masterpiece. It's about understanding your money flow, setting goals, and steering toward financial success. So, go ahead, craft that budget, and watch your financial story transform. The journey is yours, and the budget is your trusty guide. Onward to financial greatness!

Prioritizing Essential Expenses over Discretionary Spending

Alright, budgeting pros, let's talk about the art of prioritizing and adjusting—like the conductor of your financial orchestra. Ready to fine-tune your budgeting skills? Let's roll!

Prioritize Essential Expenses

Imagine your budget as a concert, and essential expenses are the main performers. Before diving into the encore of discretionary spending, allocate funds for necessities like rent, utilities, and groceries. These are the rockstars that get the stage first, ensuring your financial symphony starts on a strong note.

Let's say your earnings are $200, and your necessities like rent and utilities total $120. Before hitting the discretionary spending beats, allocate that $120 to essentials. This ensures your financial rhythm is steady and you're taking care of your must-haves first.

Steps to Adjusting Budget Strategies

In the truest sense of things, life is a dynamic concert, and sometimes the tune changes. Here are some strategies to tweak your budget when circumstances make things go out of harmony; we will sample scenarios and strategies for different contexts.

1. Fluctuating Income

Scenario: Your part-time job hours vary each month.

Strategy: Create a budget based on the minimum expected income. If you earn more, allocate the extra to savings or discretionary spending. It's like harmonizing with the ups and downs of your income.

2. Unexpected Expenses

Scenario: Surprise car repair or a sudden medical expense.

Strategy: Create an emergency fund category in your budget. When unexpected expenses pop up, allocate funds from this category. It's like having a financial safety net for life's unexpected solos.

3. New Income Source

Scenario: You start freelancing and earn extra income.

Strategy: Consider allocating a percentage of this new income to savings or a specific financial goal. It's like adding a new instrument to your financial orchestra, creating richer tunes.

4. Recurring Expenses Change

Scenario: Your internet bill increases unexpectedly.

Strategy: Reevaluate your budget categories. If one expense rises, find ways to adjust others to maintain balance. It's like keeping the harmony intact when one instrument gets louder.

5. Unexpected Windfalls

Scenario: Birthday money or unexpected gifts.

Strategy: Consider allocating a portion to savings or fun discretionary spending. It's like adding a delightful surprise note to your budget, enhancing your financial melody.

Adjusting your budget is like fine-tuning a musical masterpiece. It ensures your financial composition stays in harmony with life's unexpected realities. When you prioritize essentials and adapt your budget as circumstances sway, you become the maestro of your financial symphony, orchestrating success and resilience. Keep playing on budgeting virtuosos!

Monitoring and Adjusting Budgets

Let's talk about the crucial skill of monitoring and adjusting budgets—it's like giving your financial game plan a regular check-up to ensure it stays strong and healthy. Ready to dive in? Let's roll!

Importance of Regular Review

Think of your budget like a dynamic strategy game. Regularly reviewing it is like scanning the battlefield to make sure you're on the winning path. When you consistently do this, you stay in control, adapt to changes, and keep marching toward your financial victory.

Analyzing Spending Patterns and Identifying Areas for Adjustment

Imagine your spending patterns as the characters in your financial story. Regularly observing them helps you understand the plot and make informed decisions. Are certain categories consistently high? Are there areas where you consistently underspend? Analyzing these patterns is like decoding the storyline of your budget.

Scenarios

You notice your entertainment expenses are consistently higher than expected. It's like recognizing a recurring trait in your finances. When you note this pattern, you can make conscious choices to cut back and reallocate funds.

On the flip side, maybe your grocery spending is consistently under budget. This is like a subplot in your financial story. You can decide to reallocate some of those saved funds to a savings goal or another area that needs attention.

Now, let's talk about making adjustments. Life is full of surprises, and your budget needs to adapt. Identifying areas where you can cut back or reallocate funds is like tweaking your gameplay to overcome challenges.

Let's assume that your subscription costs for streaming services are higher than expected. It's like an unexpected turn in your financial road. You can decide to cut back on certain services or find more budget-friendly alternatives, freeing up funds for other priorities.

In another event, assume your transportation expenses are consistently lower than budgeted. This is like discovering an unexpected ally in your financial journey. You can choose to reallocate those extra funds to boost your savings or invest in another financial goal.

Tips for Successful Monitoring and Adjustment

1. **Set Regular Check-Ins**: Schedule monthly or quarterly check-ins with your budget. It's like staying vigilant in your financial strategy game.
2. **Celebrate Progress**: When you successfully cut back or reallocate funds, celebrate your victories. It's like unlocking achievements in your financial storyline.
3. **Stay Flexible**: Life is unpredictable. Be ready to adapt your budget when unexpected events occur. It's like having a dynamic script for your financial adventure.

Monitoring and adjusting your budget is like refining your game strategy. When you regularly review spending patterns and make informed adjustments, you become the master strategist of your financial journey. Stay proactive, stay adaptive, and keep leveling up toward your financial goals. Onward to victory, budgeting champions!

Tips for Staying Motivated and Disciplined in Sticking to Your Budget

Alright, budgeting champions, let's talk about the secrets to staying motivated and disciplined in the budgeting game. In finance, areas like sticking to budgeting could be boring and difficult to be consistent with. For this reason, you need to stay motivated on this course to keep your financial adventure thrilling and rewarding. Ready to level up? Let's roll!

Tips for Staying Motivated

1. Set Achievable Milestones

Let's paint a vivid example. Let's say you set a target for yourself to conveniently do a hundred push-ups over a long period—say six months. It would make sense that the fastest way to achieve this is to break your overall goal into achievable milestones, conquering each level one by one and boosting your motivation for the next challenge.

2. Visualize Your Goals

Picture your financial goals as the end of a treasure map. Create a visual representation—like a vision board or a simple list. It's like having a roadmap that keeps you focused on the ultimate treasure at the end.

3. Reward Yourself

Treat yourself when you hit a budgeting milestone. It's like unlocking a bonus level in your financial game. Whether it's a small splurge or a fun activity, rewards make sticking to your budget more enjoyable.

4. Involve a Budgeting Buddy

Share your budgeting journey with a friend or family member. It's like having a co-op mode in your financial game. You can motivate each other, share tips, and celebrate victories together.

Tips for Discipline in Sticking to the Budget

1. Prioritize Essentials

Imagine your budget is a survival kit. Prioritize essential expenses —it's like ensuring you have enough rations for the journey. Focusing on needs first always builds a strong foundation for disciplined budgeting.

2. Stay Accountable

Share your budgeting goals with someone you trust. It's like having a mentor in your financial adventure. Regular check-ins create a sense of accountability, encouraging you to stay disciplined.

3. Review and Reflect

Treat your budget like a reflection in a mirror. Regularly review your spending habits and adjust accordingly. It's like keeping your financial image sharp and clear, promoting discipline.

Recommendations for Budgeting Calculators

1. Teen Budget Calculator

This calculator is tailored for teens; it's like your personal budgeting assistant. It breaks down income, expenses, and savings in a user-friendly way, helping you visualize your financial landscape (DRS, 2024).

2. Teen Budgeting Worksheet

Another tool designed with teens in mind. The interface is like the easier version of Excel that guides you through income, expenses, and savings calculations. Simple and effective for teens starting their budgeting journey.

3. Student Budget Calculator

Ideal for students navigating the complexities of budgeting. It's like having a budgeting tutor at your fingertips. This calculator considers student-specific expenses, making it a valuable tool for those in the academic realm.

As we wrap up this chapter, consider these resounding quotes:

> *"The budget is not just a collection of numbers, but an expression of our values and aspirations."*

Jack Lew (Quote, 2024)

> *"A budget is telling your money where to go instead of wondering where it went."*

Dave Ramsey (Ramsy, 2024)

> *"Do not save what is left after spending, but spend what is left after saving."*

Warren Buffett (Konak, 2023)

Remember, staying motivated and disciplined in budgeting is like powering up in a game—it leads to financial victories.

As we wrap up our budgeting adventure, remain conscious that budgeting is the foundation of your financial success story. Now, let's venture into the next chapter, Chapter 5. Here, we'll delve into the world of borrowing and debt management, building on the solid groundwork laid by your budgeting skills. Get ready to equip yourself with the tools necessary to overcome the complexities of loans and debts, armed with the wisdom gained from mastering your budget. The journey continues!

Interactive Questions

1. What is the primary purpose of regularly reviewing your budget?

    a) To create stress
    b) To adapt to changes
    c) To complicate financial matters
    d) To avoid financial success

2. What does prioritizing essential expenses involve?

    a) Ignoring essential needs
    b) Allocating funds for necessities first
    c) Spending recklessly on nonessentials
    d) Setting unrealistic savings goals

3. How can you visualize your financial goals for better motivation?

    a) Ignore your goals
    b) Create a vision board
    c) Forget about rewards
    d) Share your goals with no one

4. What is the purpose of a budgeting calculator?

    a) To complicate budgeting
    b) To make budgeting easier
    c) To predict the future
    d) To confuse financial goals

5. Why is staying accountable important in budgeting?

    a) It's unnecessary
    b) It promotes discipline
    c) It hinders progress
    d) It's time-consuming

6. What is the significance of celebrating milestones in budgeting?

    a) To discourage progress
    b) To ignore achievements
    c) To boost motivation
    d) To complicate financial goals

Fascinating Facts

1. Did you know that the concept of budgeting dates back to ancient civilizations? The Roman Empire, for instance, had a detailed system to manage finances and allocate resources efficiently (Hossein, 2023).
2. The famous playwright William Shakespeare once said, "Neither a borrower nor a lender be." This timeless advice emphasizes the importance of thoughtful borrowing and lending (Tearle 2021).

FIVE

Navigate Borrowing and Debt

Have you ever wondered how to make informed borrowing decisions without drowning in debt? This chapter holds the key to understanding borrowing options, managing debt wisely, and building credit responsibly. First, we're diving into the world of borrowing and debt—an essential part of adulting responsibly with your finances.

In this chapter, we'll equip you with the skills to make smart borrowing decisions, manage debt like a pro, and build a solid credit history. By the end of this journey, you'll have the tools to navigate the world of finance with confidence and clarity.

Understanding Borrowing Options

First things first, you might be thinking, "Borrowing? Isn't that for adults?" Well, yes and no. Teens like you have borrowing options, too, and it's essential to understand them.

Types of Borrowing Options

Let's start by understanding borrowing options. Yep, you heard it right—there's more than one way to borrow money, and each comes with its own set of pros and cons. But don't worry, we're here to guide you through it step by step, like a trusty GPS for your finances.

Now, let's break it down further. When it comes to borrowing, you've got options like:

1. **Student Loans:** Perfect for funding your education dreams without breaking the bank upfront.
2. **Credit Cards**: Handy for covering unexpected expenses, but remember to use them wisely and pay off the balance in full to avoid hefty interest charges.
3. **Personal Loans:** Useful for big-ticket items like a car or home renovations, but make sure you understand the terms and repayment schedule before signing on the dotted line.
4. **Payday Loans:** A quick fix for short-term cash needs, but beware—the interest rates can be sky-high, so only use them in emergencies.

About personal loans or payday loans? Well, hold your horses! These options can be risky, especially for teens. As mentioned earlier, personal loans often come with high-interest rates, and payday loans can quickly spiral into a debt trap. We're all about helping you make smart choices with your money, and these options might not be the best fit for teens like you.

Let's talk about Sarah and Jake. They're like real-life financial teen superheroes, each using a different borrowing option to tackle their money missions.

Sarah—she's a lot like you, juggling school, friends, and maybe even a part-time job. She got strapped on her student loan cape to soar through college. With tuition fees soaring higher than a superhero in flight, Sarah knew she needed some extra financial muscle. So, she turned to a student loan. It helped her cover those hefty college bills while she focused on her studies. Thanks to responsible borrowing, Sarah graduated with flying colors and minimal financial stress.

Just like Sarah, many teens use student loans to fund their college education. It's a smart investment in your future, but remember, only borrow what you need and understand the terms before signing on the dotted line.

Now, let's swing over to Jake. When life threw unexpected expenses his way, Jake didn't panic. Instead, he reached for his trusty credit card. But hold up; this isn't a tale of reckless spending. Jake used his credit card wisely, only swiping it for emergencies like a busted laptop or a surprise vet bill for his furry sidekick.

So, there you go about credit cards: they're not free money. Jake knew that and used his card wisely, paying off the balance in full each month to avoid those pesky interest charges. It's all about balance and discipline when it comes to credit cards.

What's the takeaway here? Borrowing money isn't a one-size-fits-all deal. Yes, we're saying this again—each borrowing option has its own set of risks and rewards. So, whether it's a student loan, a credit card, or something else entirely, it's essential to choose the right borrowing option for your needs and wield it like a true money maestro. Always consider the terms, interest rates, and repayment plans before making any decisions. And always, always borrow responsibly.

So buckle up, fellow financial explorers, as we embark on this borrowing adventure together. Think of it as a choose-your-own-adventure book, but with fewer dragons and more dollars. We'll walk you through each scenario, pointing out the dark alleys and potential pitfalls along the way, helping you navigate the borrowing maze like a pro. Let's do this!

Interest Rates, Fees, and Repayment Terms Associated with Borrowing

Alright, let's break down the nitty-gritty of interest rates, fees, and repayment terms associated with borrowing in a way that's crystal clear.

Imagine you're in the market for a car, and you need a loan to make it happen. You find two lenders offering loans with different interest rates: one at 5% and the other at 10%. Now, let's crunch some numbers.

With the 5% interest rate, if you borrow $10,000 for the car, you'll end up paying $500 in interest over the course of a year. However, with the 10% interest rate, the interest shoots up to $1,000 for the same loan amount. That's double the interest just because of the rate difference!

But wait, there's more. Some lenders may also slap on additional fees, like application fees or origination fees, which can add to the total cost of borrowing. So, always read the fine print and watch out for those sneaky fees.

Now, let's talk repayment terms. This refers to how long you have to repay the loan and the frequency of payments. Longer loan terms may seem appealing because they come with lower monthly payments, but they also mean paying more in interest over time. Shorter terms, on the other hand, mean higher monthly payments but less interest paid overall.

Importance of Borrowing Responsibly and Avoiding Excessive Debt

From all we've mentioned above, here's the kicker: borrowing responsibly means understanding your financial limits and not biting off more than you can chew. Sure, it might be tempting to splurge on that dream vacation or the latest gadgets, but racking up excessive debt can quickly spiral out of control.

Take Sally, for example. She maxed out her credit cards on shopping sprees and fancy dinners, thinking she could pay them off later. But with high-interest rates and hefty monthly payments, she found herself drowning in debt and struggling to make ends meet.

On the flip side, there's Crowdy. He set a budget, lived within his means, and only borrowed what he needed for essentials like education and housing. By being disciplined and responsible with his borrowing, Crowdy avoided the debt trap and built a solid financial foundation for the future.

So, dear teens, remember: borrowing is a tool, not a free pass to splurge. Use it wisely, understand the terms, and always think long-term. Because when it comes to your financial future, every decision counts.

Managing Debt Wisely

Welcome to the next stop on our financial journey: managing debt wisely. When it comes to debt, it's not about avoiding it entirely but rather knowing how to handle it like a pro. First up, let's talk about creating a repayment plan. Picture this: You've got student loans, a credit card balance, and maybe even a personal loan. It can feel overwhelming, but fear not! We're here to help you tackle it step-by-step.

Strategies for Managing Existing Debt

One popular strategy is the **Debt Snowball Method**. Here's how it works: list all your debts from smallest to largest, regardless of interest rate. Then, focus on paying off the smallest debt first while making minimum payments on the rest. Once that's paid off, roll the money you were putting toward the smallest debt into tackling the next smallest debt. It's like a snowball rolling downhill, gaining momentum as you go.

Now, let's say you're more of a numbers person. Enter the **Debt Avalanche Method.** With this strategy, you prioritize debts based on interest rates. Start by paying off the debt with the highest interest rate first while still making minimum payments on the others. Once that's taken care of, move on to the debt with the next highest interest rate. By tackling high-interest debt first, you'll save money on interest in the long run.

But what if you're feeling overwhelmed and don't know where to start? That's where a **Debt Management Plan** comes in. This involves working with a credit counseling agency to create a personalized plan for managing your debts. They'll negotiate with creditors on your behalf to lower interest rates and create a manageable repayment schedule. It's like having a financial coach in your corner, guiding you toward debt-free living.

Lastly, let's talk about **Debt Consolidation.** This involves combining multiple debts into a single loan with a lower interest rate. It simplifies your payments and can potentially save you money on interest. Just be sure to crunch the numbers and make sure it's the right move for your financial situation.

Now, let's bring it all together with an example. Imagine you have student loans, a car loan, and credit card debt. You decide to use the Debt Snowball Method to tackle your debts, starting with the smallest balance first. As you pay off each debt, you gain momentum and motivation to keep going until you're finally debt-free.

So, dear teens, whether you're rolling with the snowball or conquering the avalanche, remember: managing debt wisely is key to financial freedom. With a solid plan and determination, you've got this!

Let's take a cue from these stories of some teens.

You know, student loans might prevent you from ever owning a home, but it doesn't have to be that way. This is where the story of Brianna Sullivan revolves.

Sullivan, who lives in Ohio, graduated in 2014 with over $16,000 in student debt. But guess what? She just closed on her first home. This is how she did it.

One year after graduation, Sullivan came across the biweekly payments approach for paying off her student debts while doing some online research. By dividing her monthly payment in half and paying it every other week, she was able to pay off her loans one year earlier.

So, when it came time for Sullivan to prepare for a down payment on a house, she was able to make interest-only student loan payments while still making progress on her overall debt.

Sullivan also used a homeowner's grant to finance 4% of her down payment. That meant she was able to cover her own $7,000 upfront costs, which included one percent of the down payment, closing costs, insurance, and inspections, while also paying down her school loans. To date, she has paid down $2,500.

Sullivan also used smart segmented budgeting, automatic payments, and her design abilities to create money on the side so she could close on her home while also paying off her college loans.

When she was asked for advice from anyone in a similar situation, she replied,

"Let your budget be your guide."

(McNay, 2017)

Let's look at another story from Lylia Rose, who recounts her experience.

"In my younger years, I dealt with a debt issue. The debt was entirely reckless, and it accumulated from the time I turned eighteen and gained access to credit until I was nineteen. It was a frenetic couple of years of extravagant spending for a variety of reasons.

Ultimately, I was living a lifestyle that my shop assistant salary at the time could not support. I went out partying several times a week, drove a car I didn't need, and had high cell phone expenses.

I acquired a shopping addiction and purchased clothes virtually every day. I attempted to fill a gap within myself by purchasing new clothes to make me feel better. If I didn't have any money and wanted to accomplish anything, I'd acquire a loan, boost my overdraft, or use a credit card. I owed £17,500 in less than two years before turning twenty.

Suddenly, I realized I was in trouble. I could not afford all of the payments. I was frightened of debt collectors and court dates, and I wanted to sort out my mess.

Fortunately, I received immediate guidance from CAB and began a debt management plan with PayPlan in 2004. It took a little over five years, but I paid back every penny on the strictest budget I'd ever had.

Essentially, PayPlan took every spare penny I had after my rent and expenses, other than a very small amount that I was left with for food and anything else I needed.

It was one of the most important things I'd ever learned, as well as one of the most stressful and dismal periods of my life."

When asked to lend her piece of advice to other teens, she said,

"Please do not suffer in silence if you are struggling with debt. Seek advice; there are lots out there to help you."

(Rose, 2024)

Consequences of Defaulting on Loans and the Impact on Credit Scores

Let's delve into the consequences of defaulting on loans and the importance of maintaining a good credit score, along with resources to seek help if needed.

Imagine you've missed a few payments on your student loans or credit card bills. It might not seem like a big deal at first, but defaulting on loans can have serious repercussions. Not only will you face late fees and penalty charges, but it can also wreak havoc on your credit score.

Your credit score is like your financial report card, and defaulting on loans can send it plummeting. A low credit score makes it harder to qualify for future loans, rent an apartment, or even land a job. It's a red flag to lenders and can haunt you for years to come.

But fear not! If you find yourself struggling with debt repayment, there are resources available to help you get back on track.

Resources for Seeking Help and Guidance If Struggling with Debt Repayment

Reach out to a trusted adult, like a parent or guardian, for guidance and support. They can offer advice on managing your finances and navigating repayment options.

You can also consider existing programs like the Student Debt Relief, the Financial Assistance Program, or the Child Welfare Capacity Building Collaborative (Assistance, 2023).

Additionally, consider seeking help from nonprofit credit counseling agencies. These organizations offer free or low-cost services to help you create a repayment plan, negotiate with creditors, and regain control of your finances. These companies recognize the burden that student loan debt can have on individuals and are offering solutions to ease the financial strain. Partnering with these companies can help you receive assistance in paying off student loans through various means, such as employer contributions, refinancing options, or even cash bonuses.

Some examples of these companies include Fidelity Investments, which offers an employer contribution program for its employees' student loan payments; SoFi, which provides refinancing services if you're looking to lower your monthly payments and interest rates; and Chegg, which offers a scholarship program that awards cash prizes toward outstanding student loans (Tretina & Hannah, 2021).

Online resources like financial literacy websites and forums can also provide valuable information and support. From budgeting tips to debt management strategies, there's a wealth of knowledge at your fingertips.

Dear teenager, facing financial challenges is nothing to be ashamed of. Reach out for help and take proactive steps to address your debt, and you're taking control of your financial future and setting yourself up for success. You've got this!

Building Credit Responsibly

Welcome to the next leg of our financial journey: Building Credit Responsibly. Buckle up because we're diving into the world of credit scores and why they matter.

Importance of Building a Positive Credit History and Maintaining a Good Credit Score

First things first, let's talk about the importance of building a positive credit history and maintaining a good credit score. Think of your credit score as your financial reputation. It tells lenders how reliable you are with borrowing money and paying it back on time. A good credit score opens doors to better loan terms, lower interest rates, and even approval for things like renting an apartment or getting a cell phone plan.

How Credit Scores Are Calculated and the Factors That Influence Creditworthiness

Now, onto the burning question: *How Is My Credit Score Calculated?*

Your credit score is calculated using a mathematical formula that takes into account several factors. While the exact formula is a closely guarded secret, we do know that the main factors that influence your creditworthiness include:

1. **Payment History**: This is the most important factor and accounts for about 35% of your credit score. It shows whether you've paid your bills on time and in full. Missing

payments or making late payments can significantly lower your score.

2. **Credit Utilization**: This refers to the amount of credit you're using compared to the total amount available to you. Ideally, you should aim to keep your credit utilization below 30% to maintain a healthy score.

3. **Length of Credit History**: The length of time you've had credit accounts accounts for about 15% of your score. Generally, the longer you've had credit accounts in good standing, the better it is for your score.

4. **Credit Mix**: Lenders like to see a mix of different types of credit, such as credit cards, loans, and mortgages. Having a diverse credit portfolio can positively impact your score.

5. **New Credit**: Opening multiple new credit accounts in a short period of time can signal financial distress and lower your score. Be mindful of how often you apply for new credit.

6. **Credit Inquiries**: When you apply for credit, lenders may perform a hard inquiry on your credit report, which can temporarily ding your score. Limit unnecessary credit inquiries to maintain a healthy score.

Understanding these factors and practicing responsible credit habits can help you build and maintain a positive credit history. Pay your bills on time, keep your credit utilization low, and only apply for credit when necessary. With patience and diligence, you'll be well on your way to mastering the art of building credit responsibly.

Strategies for Establishing Credit Responsibly

Alright, let's talk about strategies for establishing credit responsibly and hear some inspiring success stories from fellow teens like yourself!

First off, using credit cards wisely can be a game-changer when it comes to building credit. It's like dipping your toe into the credit pool before diving in headfirst. Start by getting a credit card with a low limit and making small, manageable purchases that you can easily pay off in full each month. This shows lenders that you're responsible and can handle credit responsibly.

Now, let's shine the spotlight on some real-life success stories. Meet Meyer Mellers, a nineteen-year-old college student who got her first credit card and used it to build her credit history. She made sure to only charge what she could afford, and she always paid her bills on time. Thanks to her smart credit habits, Mia now has a solid credit score and is on her way to financial independence.

Or how about Ronn Davies, a high school senior who used a secured credit card to establish his credit history? Despite being young, Davies understood the importance of building credit early on. He used his card for small purchases like gas and groceries, then paid off the balance in full each month. His dedication paid off, and now Davies has a bright financial future ahead of him.

Note this quote by Mark Cuban:

"Pay off your debt first. Freedom from debt is worth more than any amount you can earn."

(Sather, 2023)

You can check out these resource links to debt payoff calculators and credit score simulators for easy access and utilization.

Debt Payoff Calculator

1. Debt Payoff Calculator (https://www.calculator.net/)

The calculator below estimates the amount of time required to pay back one or more debts. Additionally, it gives users the most cost-efficient payoff sequence, with the option of adding extra payments. This calculator utilizes the debt avalanche method, which is considered the most cost-efficient payoff strategy from a financial perspective.

2. Debt Snowball Calculator (https://www.ramseysolutions.com/debt/debt-calculator)

The debt snowball is a debt payoff method where you pay your debts from smallest to largest, regardless of interest rate. Knock out the smallest debt first. Then, take what you were paying on that debt and add it to the payment of your next smallest debt.

Its philosophy is that—just like a snowball rolling downhill—paying off debt is all about momentum. With every debt you pay off, you gain speed until you're an unstoppable, debt-crushing force.

3. Debt Payoff Calculator x 2 (https://www.congressionalfcu.org/services/calculators/debt-payoff-calculator)

The Congressional Federal has been committed to helping the people who serve on Capitol Hill achieve their financial goals via transition loans that help members move through each stage of their lives. They provide education and offer great financial solutions with member-focused personal service to ensure you get all the products you expect with all the service you deserve—no matter what your financial dreams might be.

Credit Score Simulator

1. Credit Score Simulator (https://www.creditkarma.com/)

The Credit Score Simulator starts with the information in your current TransUnion credit report and explores how changing that information could affect your score. Of course, it's all hypothetical. Simulating these changes won't actually affect your score or report.

The Credit Score Simulator is an educational tool. Explore, adjust, and ponder, but just remember that these are estimated outcomes and not predictions.

2. Fico Score Estimator (https://www.myfico.com/)

myFICO makes it easy to understand your credit with FICO scores, credit reports, and alerts from all 3 bureaus (Experian, TransUnion, and Equifax).

Knowing your FICO score helps you apply for loans with confidence and avoid surprises.

Interactive Questions

Now, let's test your knowledge with some interactive questions:

1. What is the most important factor in calculating your credit score?

  a) Length of Credit History
  b) Credit Utilization
  c) Payment History
  d) Credit Mix

2. What is the recommended credit utilization ratio to maintain a healthy credit score?

a) 50%
b) 30%
c) 70%
d) 10%

3. What strategy involves paying off the smallest debt first and then rolling the payments into the next smallest debt?

a) Debt Avalanche Method
b) Debt Snowball Method
c) Debt Consolidation
d) Debt Management Plan

4. What is the potential consequence of defaulting on loans?

a) Lower interest rates
b) Improved credit score
c) Higher credit limit
d) Negative impact on credit score

5. What is the first step in establishing a positive credit history?

a) Applying for multiple credit cards
b) Making timely payments
c) Ignoring credit offers
d) Maxing out credit cards

6. How can teens seek help if they are struggling with debt repayment?

    a) Reach out to a trusted adult or credit counseling agency
    b) Ignore the problem and hope it goes away
    c) Apply for more loans to cover existing debt
    d) Stop making payments altogether

Fascinating Facts

Now, let's spice things up with some fascinating financial facts:

1. In Japan, there are vending machines that dispense gold bars! Talk about a golden opportunity.
2. The term "piggy bank" comes from an old English term, "pygg," which refers to a type of clay used to make jars for storing money.
3. The world's largest piggy bank was over 15 feet tall and could hold up to 30,000 coins. That's one hefty piggy!

SIX

Cultivate Savings Mindset

I magine a life where you can pursue your passions and dreams without constantly worrying about financial constraints. Picture being able to travel, start a business, or pursue further education without the burden of debt or financial stress. This chapter holds the key to unlocking that freedom by teaching you how to save wisely and build a secure financial foundation for your future.

Importance of Savings

Picture this: You've got a stash of cash tucked away for a rainy day. It's like having a safety net that cushions you from life's unexpected curveballs. Yes, you've got to see it beyond just stashing cash under your mattress. That's the magic of saving money—it gives you peace of mind and financial preparedness for whatever comes your way.

But wait, there's more because saving isn't just about preparing for emergencies; it's also about setting yourself up for success in the long run. Let's break it down!

Benefits of Saving Money

1. **Financial Preparedness**: Saving money ensures you're ready to tackle unexpected expenses, like a broken phone or a surprise medical bill. It's like having your own superhero cape when life throws a curveball your way.

2. **Compound Growth**: Have you ever heard of the saying "time is money?" Well, when it comes to saving, time is your best friend. The secret of compound interest is starting early and letting your money grow over time. In doing this, you're setting yourself up for financial success down the road. And you know what? You've got the time now that you're a teen. Take advantage!

3. **Safety from Economic Downturns**: Economic ups and downs are inevitable, but having a solid savings cushion can help you weather the storm with ease. It's like having a sturdy umbrella that shields you from the financial rain.

4. **Setting a Great Example**: Saving money isn't just about you; it's also about setting a positive example for future generations. Whether it's your siblings, friends, or future children, showing them the importance of saving instills lifelong financial habits.

5. **Reap Its Rewards Come Retirement**: It may seem light-years away, but saving money now means you'll be able to enjoy a comfortable retirement later. It's like planting seeds today to enjoy a bountiful harvest in the future.

So, dear teens, as you embark on your savings journey, remind yourself that every dollar saved is a step closer to financial security, achieving your goals, and building wealth over time. Get ready to flex your saving muscles and watch your financial future flourish!

Paying Yourself First and Automating Savings Contributions

Ever heard of the concept of paying yourself first? It's like putting on your own oxygen mask before helping others on a plane. When you pay yourself first, you prioritize saving money before anything else. It's a simple but powerful strategy that ensures you're always putting your financial well-being first. Think of it as treating your future self to a little financial TLC before tackling your other expenses.

Now, let's talk about automating savings contributions. It's like setting up a piggy bank that fills itself up without you even having to think about it. Automating your savings makes it effortless to sock away money for your goals. Whether it's setting up automatic transfers from your checking account to your savings account or enrolling in a workplace retirement plan, automation takes the guesswork out of saving and helps you stay on track.

Short-Term and Long-Term Savings Goals to Inspire Savings

At the very basic level, savings goals come in two categories: short-term and long-term.

Long-term goals are things you want to achieve in the future, usually over a period of several years. Short-term goals, on the other hand, are things you want to achieve in the near future, usually within a year or less. Let's dive deeper.

Short-Term Savings Goals

Alright, let's get inspired with some short-term savings goals! Imagine you've got a pesky credit card debt hanging over your head. Setting a goal to pay it off can feel like conquering a mountain. By creating a budget and sticking to it religiously, you'll chip away at that debt faster than you ever thought possible.

Or how about opening a checking account with no fees? It's like finding a treasure chest full of gold coins waiting to be discovered. If you ditch those pesky fees, you'll keep more of your hard-earned money where it belongs—in your pocket.

And let's not forget about finding ways to earn extra money through part-time jobs or selling items online. It's like planting seeds in a garden and watching them grow into a bountiful harvest. Hustling and finding creative ways to boost your income could supercharge your savings and help you reach your goals in no time.

Long-Term Savings Goals

Now, let's dream big with some long-term savings goals! Picture yourself investing in stocks or mutual funds, as we discussed in earlier chapters. It's like planting a money tree that grows taller and taller with each passing year. Investing early and consistently could help you harness the power of compounding and watch your wealth grow exponentially over time.

Or how about building an emergency fund? It's like building a fortress to protect yourself from life's unexpected events. If, for example, you set aside enough money to cover three to six months' worth of expenses, you'll have peace of mind knowing that you're financially prepared for whatever comes your way.

And last but not least, starting a retirement savings plan. It's like building a time machine that allows you to travel into the future and live your best life. The hack? Start early and contribute regularly to a retirement account, and you'll set yourself up for a comfortable and fulfilling retirement down the road.

Strategies for Saving Money

Alright, let's learn some practical strategies for saving money, like budgeting for savings, reducing expenses, and avoiding lifestyle inflation, all of which will have you feeling like a financial wizard in no time!

Practical Tips and Tricks for Saving Money

1. **Open the Right Bank Account**: Look for a savings account with a high-interest rate and no fees to maximize your savings potential.
2. **Set a Savings Goal with the 52-Week Challenge**: It's like embarking on a treasure hunt with a map to guide you. Start small by saving $1 in week one, then increase your savings by $1 each week. By the end of the year, you'll have saved over $1,300 without even breaking a sweat.
3. **Practice the 30-Day Rule to Prevent Impulse Purchases**: Imagine you're window shopping and spot a shiny new gadget that you just have to have. Instead of splurging on the spot, give yourself 30 days to think it over. You'll be surprised at how many impulse buys you'll avoid by simply waiting it out.
4. **Hide Your Debit Card and Pay with Cash**: It's like putting a lock on the cookie jar to resist temptation. You'd find that using cash for your everyday purchases may make you more mindful of your spending and less likely to overspend.
5. **Make a Cash-Match Pact with Your Parents**: It's like having a financial cheerleader in your corner. Ask your parents to match a portion of your savings each month as an extra incentive to save.

6. **Embrace Student Discounts (They Add Up Fast)**: Think of it like finding buried treasure wherever you go. From movie tickets to clothing stores, take advantage of student discounts to stretch your dollars further.

7. **Pay Yourself First**: Picture yourself as a savvy CEO, taking a cut of the profits before divvying up the rest. Set up automatic transfers from your checking account to your savings account each month to prioritize saving.

8. **Find a Budget That Works for You**: Whether you prefer a spreadsheet or a budgeting app, find a budgeting method that fits your lifestyle and stick to it religiously.

9. **Automate Your Savings**: It's like setting your savings on autopilot and watching your money grow effortlessly. Schedule automatic transfers from your paycheck to your savings account to ensure consistent savings each month.

10. **Buckle Down with a Part-Time Job**: Imagine yourself as a money-making machine, churning out cash with every shift. Whether it's babysitting, dog walking, or working at your local coffee shop, a part-time job can turbocharge your savings and give you valuable work experience.

The Role of Emergency Funds in Providing a Financial Safety Net for Unexpected Expenses

Now, let's talk about emergency funds. Think of it like a firefighter who swoops in to save the day when a from-the-blue event occurs. An emergency fund is like a financial safety net that provides peace of mind, knowing that you're prepared for unexpected expenses, like car repairs or medical bills. By setting aside up to three or six months' worth of expenses in a separate savings account, you'll be ready to tackle whatever life throws your way without breaking a sweat. So start building your emergency fund today and rest easy knowing that you're financially prepared for whatever comes your way!

Exploring Different Saving Methods

Ready to take your savings game to the next level? Let's explore some different saving methods that'll transform you into a financial rockstar in no time!

First up, we've got traditional savings accounts. Think of them like a trusty piggy bank—a safe and reliable place to stash your cash. These accounts are great for short-term savings goals and emergencies, offering easy access to your money whenever you need it.

Next, let's talk about high-yield savings accounts. Picture them as turbocharged piggy banks offering higher interest rates than traditional savings accounts. This means your money grows faster over time, helping you reach your goals even sooner. Plus, they're still just as safe and accessible as traditional accounts.

But wait, there's more! Ever heard of investment accounts? With investment accounts, you're not just saving—you're putting your money to work by investing in stocks, bonds, or mutual funds. While there's more risk involved compared to savings accounts, the potential for higher returns makes it an exciting option for long-term savings goals.

So, dear teen, whether you're saving for a rainy day, your dream vacation, or even retirement down the road, there's a saving method out there that's perfect for you. Take the time to explore your options, weigh the pros and cons, and choose the method that best fits your financial goals and comfort level. With a little patience and diligence, you'll be well on your way to building a brighter financial future. Happy saving!

Now, let's go see some success stories of teens who implemented these strategies and saw their savings grow.

When Dawn Morgan was a teenager, she really wanted to get braces. Her parents, though, didn't have the money for it, so she had to save for them herself.

Later, in her twenties, Morgan took financial workshops to learn more about money management, including how to avoid debt and save. Now a freelance writer and filmmaker in her mid-thirties, she's in the midst of launching a Kickstarter campaign to fund a short film, *Emily's Braces*, featuring a teenage girl who learns about money by saving for braces—just as she did twenty years ago (Pamer, 2015).

For Johnnie Lovett, a young Illinois saver, saving has been a habit since he was a teenager. His parents introduced him to the concepts of budgeting, saving, and money management. He has taken that advice to heart and is now regularly saving. To deal with temptation, he saves first prior to spending. He then makes a list of the things he needs and the things she wants and gives himself a budget for both. He also keeps $200 in a separate account, not in his checking or savings, in case of emergencies.

As part of his regular savings plan, Johnnie allocates money toward his short-term and long-term goals. One of his long-term goals is to purchase a house when he graduates.

He reveals some facts that highlight his story:

> *"As a teenager, I was responsible for buying certain things with my allowance."*

(Lovett, 2024)

Maximizing Savings Potential

Onward we march; let's unlock the secrets to maximizing your savings potential and harnessing the power of compound interest to grow your money like never before!

The Power of Compound Interest

First things first, let's talk about compound interest. It's like planting a money tree and watching it grow bigger and bigger with each passing year. Here's how it works: When you save or invest your money, you earn interest not only on your initial deposit but also on the interest that accrues over time. This means your money grows exponentially, snowballing into a tidy sum over the years.

Check out this table to see the magic of compounding in action:

Year	Initial Deposit	Interest Earned (5%)	Total Balance
1	$1,000	$50	$1,050
2	$1,050	$52.50	$1,102.50
3	$1,102.50	$55.13	$1,157.63
4	$1,157.63	$57.88	$1,215.51
5	$1,215.51	$60.78	$1,276.29

As you can see, even with a modest initial deposit of $1,000 and a relatively low-interest rate of 5%, your money grows significantly over just five years, thanks to the power of compounding.

Strategies for Maximizing Your Savings Potential

Now, let's talk about strategies for maximizing your savings potential. One powerful way to supercharge your savings is by contributing to retirement accounts like a 401(k) or IRA. It's like watching your planted seeds grow into a lush oasis of wealth. The key is to start early and contribute regularly to these accounts. In doing this, you'll take advantage of tax benefits and employer-matching contributions, turbocharging your savings for retirement.

Another strategy is investing in tax-advantaged accounts like a Health Savings Account (HSA) or a 529 College Savings Plan. These accounts offer tax benefits that allow your money to grow faster compared to taxable accounts. It's like giving your money a VIP pass to the fast lane of wealth-building, helping you reach your financial goals even sooner.

So, dear teen, be sure that the power of compounding is your secret weapon for growing your money exponentially over time. Happy saving!

Setting Savings Goals and Developing a Savings Plan to Achieve Them

Alright, let's swing into setting savings goals and crafting a plan to make those dreams a reality. And guess what? We've got some inspiring stories to show you that anyone—yes, even regular folks like you and me—can achieve financial greatness through disciplined saving and investing.

First off, setting savings goals is like plotting a course for your financial journey. Whether it's saving for a dream vacation, a down payment on a house, or even retirement, having clear goals gives you something to strive for and keeps you motivated along the way.

Now, let's talk about developing a savings plan to achieve those goals. Start by identifying your short-term and long-term goals. Think of it like plotting destinations on a map—where do you want to go, and how do you plan to get there? Once you've got your goals in mind, break them down into smaller, manageable milestones, then set a timeline for achieving each milestone. It's like tackling a big project one step at a time—each small victory brings you closer to your ultimate goal. It doesn't end there. Additionally, you should create a budget to track your progress and regularly review and adjust your plan as needed. This way, you'll stay on track and reach your goals faster than you ever thought possible.

But wait, there's more! Let's draw inspiration from some real-life success stories of popular individuals who reached financial milestones through disciplined saving and investing. Take Sara Blakely, for example, the founder of Spanx. She started her business with just $5,000 in savings and grew it into a billion-dollar empire through sheer determination and smart financial management. Hear what she says:

"Right when I was running out of friends and money, Oprah called ..."

(Lake, 2024)

Be aware that Oprah is synonymous with the idea of saving.

Take Jay-Z, for example. Before he became a music mogul and business tycoon, he was just a kid from Brooklyn with a dream. Through saving and investing his earnings wisely, Jay-Z built a financial empire that extends far beyond the music industry (Adeodun, 2023).

How about Chris Sacca, a former Google executive turned venture capitalist? He built his fortune through savvy investments in companies like Twitter and Uber, proving that anyone can achieve financial success with the right mindset and strategy. His words read:

"It became obvious to me that the investing side was where the action was."

(Konrad, 2015)

Forbes – Savings Goal Calculator

Check out this savings goal calculator to create your personalized savings plan.

The Forbes Savings Goal Calculator is a tool that can help you figure out how much money you need to save each month in order to reach your financial goals. It takes into account factors such as your current savings, the amount of time you have until your goal date, and the interest rate on any investments or accounts where you plan to put your savings. By inputting this information, the calculator will provide an estimate of how much money you should aim to save each month in order to reach your desired financial target by the deadline. This tool can be useful for anyone who has specific monetary objectives they want to achieve but may not know exactly how much they need to save each month in order to get there (Batdorf, 2023).

Now, as you reflect on your newfound knowledge and skills in cultivating a robust savings mindset, feel empowered to take control of your financial future. You've armed yourself with the tools and strategies to make your dreams a reality, and there's no stopping you now.

But guess what? Your journey is far from over. In the next chapter, we'll dive into practical steps for financial management and goal achievement, equipping you with the confidence and know-how to navigate your financial journey with ease. So get ready to take the next step toward financial freedom and success—you've got this!

Interactive Questions

1. What is one benefit of using a high-yield savings account?

    a) Higher interest rates
    b) Lower fees
    c) Access to investment options
    d) No withdrawal limits
    e) None of the above

2. Which strategy can help prevent impulse purchases?

    a) Automating savings
    b) Using cash instead of debit cards
    c) Opening a checking account with no fees
    d) Embracing student discounts
    e) None of the above

3. What is one advantage of contributing to retirement accounts?

    a) Tax benefits
    b) Lower risk
    c) Higher liquidity
    d) Immediate access to funds
    e) None of the above

Fascinating Facts

1. The average cost of attending a four-year public college in the United States is over $20,000 per year.
2. The term "budget" originated from the French word "bougette," which means a small bag or purse.
3. The stock market has historically provided an average annual return of around 10%.
4. The term "millionaire" was first coined in the eighteenth century by British bankers to describe individuals with wealth exceeding one million pounds.

SEVEN

Empowerment through Action

T ake some time to envision yourself as the architect of your financial destiny, setting ambitious goals and charting a course toward lifelong financial success.

Through yet?

Now, get ready to take control of your financial future and embark on a journey toward lifelong financial wellness. This chapter serves as their gateway to empowerment, offering actionable insights and strategies to seize control of their finances and turn their dreams into reality.

Let's kick things off with the first subchapter.

Taking Control of Finances

It's time to take ownership of your financial future by actively managing your money. Think of it like taking the reins of a wild horse—it may seem daunting at first, but with a little know-how and determination, you'll be riding high toward your financial goals in no time. Let's see it from another angle. Taking control of your finances is like driving your own car—you're the one in the driver's seat, steering toward your destination. It's all about being proactive and intentional with your money rather than just letting it drive you. When you actively manage your money, you're taking the reins and steering your financial future in the right direction.

Resources and Tools for Organizing Financial Documents, Tracking Progress toward Goals, and Staying Informed about Personal Finances

Let's talk about some of the best financial apps for teens and young adults. Financial apps are applications or software that help you manage your money, budget, investments, and expenses using your smartphones or other devices.

If you are just starting to learn how to handle finances, these financial apps can be very helpful in tracking expenses, setting savings goals, monitoring credit scores, investing in stocks or mutual funds, and even paying bills online.

Some of the websites listed in this article include:

- **MyMoney.gov**: A government website that provides information on budgeting, saving, investing, and other financial topics.
- **Mint.com**: An app that helps you track your spending and create budgets.
- **Investopedia:** A website that offers educational content on investing and personal finance.
- **Bankrate.com**: A site for comparing interest rates on loans and savings accounts (Eight, 2024).

In addition to digital tools, there are also physical resources available, such as books and board games like Monopoly, The

Game of Life, etc. These materials often feature characters or stories that help explain financial concepts in a fun way (Activities, 2022).

Others include Acorns (which helps you invest spare change from everyday purchases into diversified portfolios), Robinhood (for stock trading without paying any fees), Venmo Cash App (peer-to-peer payments), and Karma (for credit scores). These apps offer features such as personalized budgets based on income and spending habits, automatic saving options where spare change from purchases gets invested into stocks, commission-free trading of individual stocks, and easy peer-to-peer payment transfers between friends (Activities, 2018).

Overall, these financial tools provide an accessible way to manage personal finance while also learning about investing strategies at a younger age.

Making Informed Decisions

Now, let's talk about making informed financial decisions. Imagine you're at a crossroads, trying to decide between spending your money on a new pair of shoes or saving it for a rainy day. If you understand the true value of your money, weigh the pros and cons of each decision, and prioritize your financial goals, you'll make choices that align with your future financial well-being.

But wait, there's more!

Tips and Tools for Organizing Financial Documents and Tracking Progress

Let's talk about organizing financial documents. It's like tidying up your room—a little bit of organization goes a long way in reducing stress and helping you stay on top of your finances. Start by creating a filing system for important documents like bank statements, tax returns, and insurance policies. Consider using digital tools like budgeting apps or spreadsheets to track your income and expenses, making it easier to monitor your progress toward your financial goals.

Now, let's arm you with some practical tips and tools to make managing your money a breeze:

1. **Create a Budget**: This helps you stay on track and avoid overspending.
2. **Set Financial Goals**: Think of them like destinations on your roadmap—clear, measurable targets to strive toward.
3. **Track Your expenses**: It's like keeping tabs on your fuel gauge—you'll know when you're veering off course and can make adjustments accordingly.
4. **Build an Emergency Fund**: Think of it like a safety net for unexpected bumps in the road—you'll have peace of mind knowing you're financially prepared for whatever life throws your way.
5. **Educate yourself**: It's like upgrading your navigation system—the more you know about personal finance, the better equipped you'll be to make smart financial decisions.

So, dear teen, take control of your finances! Rev up those engines, and let's hit the road to financial empowerment! The horizon is yours to conquer!

Pursuing Financial Goals

Alright, let's dive into the exciting world of pursuing financial goals and building resilience and persistence along the way!

Developing a Clear Roadmap for Achieving Financial Goals by Identifying Specific Actions and Milestones

Imagine your financial goals as towering mountains on the horizon—daunting but totally conquerable with the right plan in place. It's all about breaking down those big, intimidating goals into smaller, more manageable steps, like climbing a staircase one step at a time.

Strategies for Breaking Down Large Goals into Smaller, Manageable Tasks and Tracking Progress

Here's how you can develop a clear roadmap for achieving your financial goals:

1. **Identify Specific Actions and Milestones**: Picture your goals as destinations on a map—each one marking a significant milestone on your journey to financial success. Break down your goals into smaller, actionable steps, and set clear milestones to track your progress along the way.

2. **Break Down Large Goals into Smaller Tasks:** It's like slicing a pizza into bite-sized slices—much easier to tackle one piece at a time! Break down your big goals into smaller, more manageable tasks, and focus on completing each task before moving on to the next. Before you know it, you'll have made significant progress toward your ultimate goal.

3. **Track Your Progress**: Think of it like checking your GPS to make sure you're on the right track. Keep tabs on your progress by regularly reviewing your financial goals and tracking your income, expenses, and savings. Celebrate your victories along the way and make adjustments as needed to stay on course.

But here's a thing ... Check the next point of this subchapter.

The Need for Perseverance and Resilience in the Face of Setbacks to Achieving Financial Goals

Achieving your financial goals won't always be smooth sailing. There will be obstacles and setbacks along the way, like unexpected expenses or economic downturns. That's where resilience and persistence come into play.

Resilience is like a superpower that helps you bounce back from setbacks stronger than ever. When faced with challenges, instead of giving up or getting discouraged, tap into your inner resilience and find creative solutions to overcome obstacles. Remember, every setback is an opportunity to learn and grow stronger.

Persistence is like the engine that keeps you moving forward, even when the going gets tough. It's about staying committed to your goals and pushing through adversity with determination and grit. When you encounter roadblocks or setbacks, don't throw in the towel—double down on your efforts and keep pushing forward toward your goals.

So, dear teens, as you embark on your journey to achieve your financial goals, remember resilience and persistence are your secret weapons for success. Developing a clear roadmap, breaking down your goals into manageable tasks, and embracing resilience and persistence will position you to overcome any obstacle and reach new heights of financial success. So keep dreaming big, stay focused, and never give up—your financial future is waiting for you!

Building a Lifetime of Financial Wellness

Hey there, future financial gurus! We've covered a lot of ground on your journey to financial empowerment, but the learning doesn't stop here. In fact, it's just the beginning!

The Importance of Lifelong Learning and Continuous Improvement in Financial Literacy and Skills

Lifelong learning and continuous improvement in financial literacy and skills are like the fuel that keeps your financial engine running smoothly.

Think of it like upgrading to the latest model of your favorite video game—each new level brings new challenges and opportunities for growth. Staying curious, informed, and open to learning is proven to continuously sharpen your financial skills and adapt to the ever-changing landscape of personal finance.

But here's the really cool part: as you level up your financial knowledge and skills, you have the power to pay it forward and make a difference in your community.

The Importance of Sharing Financial Knowledge and Experiences with Others

Sharing your knowledge and experiences with others fosters a culture of financial empowerment and well-being, creating a ripple effect of positive change that benefits everyone.

Imagine you're the star player on your school's basketball team, and you've just mastered a killer new move. Instead of keeping it to yourself, you share it with your teammates, helping them improve their game and achieve greater success together. Similarly, by sharing your financial knowledge and experiences with your friends, family, and peers, you're empowering them to take control of their own financial futures and build a brighter tomorrow.

Examples That Show How Financial Literacy Can Lead to Adaptability and Success In Different Life Stages

Now, let's draw inspiration from some real-life examples of how financial literacy can lead to adaptability and success in different life stages:

Take Serena Williams, for example, one of the greatest tennis players of all time. Beyond her prowess on the court, Serena has also become a savvy businesswoman, investing in ventures ranging from fashion to technology (Agenda, 224). Her financial literacy and smart investing have helped her adapt and thrive both on and off the court, proving that financial empowerment knows no bounds.

Learn from her prowess in financial literacy:

> *"I want to be a part of it. I want to be in the infrastructure. I want to be the brand, instead of just being the face."*
>
> (Badenhausen, 2019)

So, dear teen financial sensation, as you embark on your journey to build a lifetime of financial wellness, remember: the power to change your financial future and the world around you lies in your hands. Stay curious, stay informed, and stay empowered—the sky's the limit!

Community Initiatives Promoting Financial Empowerment among Teens

Let's shine a spotlight on some current community initiatives that are paving the way for financial empowerment among teens!

The first organization is the National Endowment for Financial Education (NEFE). NEFE provides educational resources and tools for individuals, educators, and professionals to improve financial decision-making.

The second organization is the Jump$tart Coalition for Personal Financial Literacy. Jump$tart's mission is to educate young people on personal finance by working with schools, businesses, and government agencies.

Next up is the Council for Economic Education (CEE), which focuses on providing economic education in schools from kindergarten through high school. CEE also offers professional development programs for teachers.

Fourth on the list is Operation HOPE, an organization that provides financial education and coaching services to underserved communities around the world. They offer programs such as credit counseling, homebuyer workshops, and entrepreneurship training.

Finally, there's Money Management International (MMI), a nonprofit credit counseling agency that helps consumers manage debt through budgeting assistance and debt management plans (Simon-Gersuk, 2024).

Another fantastic initiative is the partnership between schools and financial institutions to bring financial education directly into the classroom. From guest speakers to hands-on projects, these programs provide teens with practical knowledge and tools to navigate their financial futures with confidence!

Now, as you prepare to apply your financial wisdom to navigate major life events, tell yourself, "I've got the knowledge, skills, and resources to tackle whatever comes my way with confidence." Whether it's pursuing higher education, starting a career, buying a home, or starting a family, you're equipped to make informed decisions and build a bright future for yourself.

In the next chapter, we'll discuss practical strategies for planning and preparing for these significant milestones, helping you navigate life's transitions with ease. So get ready to put your financial skills to the test and embark on the next phase of your financial journey—you've got this!

Meanwhile, check out this goal-setting worksheet below:

Financial Goal: _____

Specific Action Steps:

1. _____
2. _____
3. _____

Milestones to Track Progress:

_____

_____

_____

Deadline for Achievement: _____

Notes/Reflections: _____

Interactive Questions

1. What is the key benefit of automating savings contributions?

   a) It reduces the need for budgeting
   b) It increases spending habits
   c) It makes saving effortless
   d) It decreases interest rates
   e) None of the above

2. What is the purpose of setting financial goals?

   a) To spend money freely
   b) To track expenses
   c) To prioritize saving and investing
   d) To avoid financial planning
   e) None of the above

3. How does compound interest affect savings over time?

   a) It decreases savings
   b) It has no effect on savings
   c) It accelerates savings growth
   d) It slows down savings growth
   e) None of the above

4. Which strategy helps in breaking down large financial goals into manageable tasks?

  a) Avoiding financial planning
  b) Procrastination
  c) Tracking progress
  d) Continuous learning
  e) None of the above

5. Why is resilience important in pursuing financial goals?

  a) To avoid financial challenges
  b) To learn from mistakes
  c) To give up easily
  d) To make impulsive decisions
  e) None of the above

6. Which type of savings account offers higher interest rates than traditional savings accounts?

  a) Checking account
  b) High-yield savings account
  c) Retirement account
  d) Investment account
  e) None of the above

7. What does the 30-day rule help prevent?

  a) Overspending
  b) Saving money
  c) Impulse purchases
  d) Budgeting
  e) None of the above

8. What is the purpose of sharing financial knowledge with others?

a) To keep secrets
b) To foster a culture of financial empowerment
c) To hide financial success
d) To discourage others
e) None of the above

9 .How does setting specific actions and milestones help in achieving financial goals?

a) It complicates the process
b) It makes goal-setting easier
c) It reduces the need for planning
d) It prevents progress tracking
e) None of the above

10. Which strategy helps build resilience and pursue financial goals?

a) Giving up easily
b) Staying committed
c) Avoiding challenges
d) Ignoring setbacks
e) None of the above

Fascinating Facts

1. The average teenager spends around $2,600 per year.
2. In the United States, the legal age to open a savings account without parental consent is eighteen.

3. The world's youngest self-made billionaire is Kylie Jenner, who made her fortune from her cosmetics company.
4. McDonald's is one of the largest toy distributors in the world, thanks to its Happy Meal toys.
5. The average American household carries over $8,000 in credit card debt.
6. The Great Depression of the 1930s led to the creation of the Federal Deposit Insurance Corporation (FDIC) to protect bank deposits.
7. The youngest person to win a Nobel Prize was Malala Yousafzai, who won the Nobel Peace Prize at age seventeen.

EIGHT

Planning for Major Life Events

A re you ready to take charge of your financial future and prepare for life's biggest milestones? In this chapter, you'll discover invaluable insights and strategies to navigate significant life events with confidence and financial readiness.

Financial Preparation for College

Hey there, future college-bound scholars! Get ready to embark on an exciting journey toward higher education, armed with the knowledge and strategies to tackle those tuition bills and living expenses like a pro.

Teen Guide for Planning and Saving for Higher Education Expenses

Planning and saving for college expenses may seem like scaling Mount Everest, but fear not—you've got this! Let's break it down step by step, using relevant experiences among teens just like you.

First off, let's talk about tuition and fees. These are like the entrance fee to the amusement park of higher education—

necessary but sometimes a bit daunting. Start by researching the cost of tuition and fees at the different colleges and universities you're interested in attending. Consider factors like in-state vs. out-of-state tuition, public vs. private institutions (choosing community colleges or state schools over private universities is proven to reduce costs), and potential financial aid opportunities.

Next up, living costs. Think of them as the snacks and souvenirs you'll need to fuel your academic adventure. Take into account expenses like housing, meals, transportation, textbooks, and other essentials. Create a budget to estimate your monthly living expenses and factor them into your overall college savings plan. Consider setting up an automatic transfer from your checking account into a separate savings account specifically designated for college expenses.

You could opt to live at home and commute as a college student. It can save thousands of dollars a year on room and board expenses. Plus, you can ditch the campus meal plan and save money by cooking at home or joining family dinners instead. And don't worry. You can still join clubs and be a part of campus life as a commuter!

Regarding saving for college, start by setting a savings goal based on your estimated college expenses and the timeline for your education. Consider opening a dedicated college savings account, like a 529 plan, where earnings on this account grow tax-free, and withdrawals made for qualified educational expenses are also tax-free. You can also consider a Coverdell Education Savings Account (ESA) to take advantage of tax benefits and maximize your savings potential. However, there are some differences between this and the 529 plan, such as contribution limits and how the funds can be used. A high-yield savings account (unlike traditional savings) could help you achieve more over time.

But what if you're still in high school or even middle school? It's never too early to start planning and saving for college! Invest in stocks and mutual funds. It's not out of place to start a small business to earn money for college expenses. Also, consider taking advantage of summer jobs or part-time work during the school year. Here's a secret: Look out for tuition reimbursement wherever you intend to work. Some companies offer tuition reimbursement for their college student employees! New discovery, yeah? So, next time you are applying for part-time jobs, filter your job search to include companies that offer a tuition reimbursement benefit. Any little bit helps, plus you'll get professional experience to add to your résumé.

Another idea is to take AP classes. Advanced Placement (AP) classes afford you the opportunity to earn college credits while you're still in high school. Now, whether or not you receive college credit depends on your AP test scores and the college you're headed for. Although you usually have to pay a small fee for the class, it's far less than the cost of a college class. Hurray! So, speak with your academic counselor to see what AP classes are available. You can also look into dual enrollment courses offered through local community colleges (Kamel, 2024). Smart meter!

There's also the Uniform Gifts/Transfers to Minors Act (UGMA/UTMA) account, which allows you to receive gifts or financial assets without having control over them until prime adulthood (Tretina & Kantrowitz, 2023). Every dollar saved now is one less dollar you'll need to borrow later.

And don't forget about financial aid opportunities! Scholarships, grants, and student loans can help bridge the gap between your savings and the cost of college. Research and apply for scholarships early and often, and fill out the Free Application for

Federal Student Aid (FAFSA) to determine your eligibility for federal financial aid programs.

As you embark on your journey toward higher education, be sure that with careful planning, diligent saving, and a little help from financial aid, you can afford higher education without having significant debt after graduation and make your college dreams a reality. Stay focused, stay determined, and don't be afraid to ask for help along the way. Your future awaits—let's make it a bright one!

Options, Implications, and Responsibilities for Financial Aids, Scholarships, and Student Loans

Let's explore options for financial aid, scholarships, and student loans.

1. **Scholarships**: See scholarships as golden tickets to the college of your dreams—they're essentially free money that you don't have to pay back. Scholarships can be merit-based, need-based, or awarded for specific talents or achievements. Explore scholarship opportunities through your school, community organizations, and online resources. For example, there are scholarships for academic achievement, sports prowess, artistic talent, community service, and more. Keep an eye out for application deadlines and requirements, and don't hesitate to apply for as many scholarships as possible.

2. **Grants**: Grants are like gifts from the heavens—they're typically awarded based on financial need and don't need to be repaid. The most common grant is the Federal Pell Grant, which is awarded to undergraduate students based on financial need. Other grants may be available through state governments, colleges, and private organizations. To

apply for grants, you'll typically need to complete the FAFSA (Free Application for Federal Student Aid) to determine your eligibility.

3. **Work-Study Programs**: Work-study programs are like part-time jobs specifically designed for college students. These programs provide opportunities for students to work on campus or in the community to earn money to help pay for college expenses. Work-study jobs may be related to your field of study or, as we said earlier, can provide valuable work experience that can enhance your resume.

4. **Federal Student Loans**: Student loans are like a double-edged sword—they can help you pay for college, but they also come with the responsibility of repayment. Federal student loans are typically more favorable than private loans, as they offer fixed interest rates, flexible repayment options, and certain protections for borrowers. Subsidized loans are based on financial need, while unsubsidized loans are available to all eligible students regardless of financial need. It's important to borrow only what you need and to understand the terms and conditions of your loans before accepting them.

Tips for Minimizing College Costs While Maximizing Financial Resources

Check out these strategic tips for minimizing college costs and maximizing financial resources.

1. **Research Financial Aid Options Early**: Start exploring financial aid options as soon as possible, preferably in your junior year of high school. This gives you time to research

scholarships, grants, and other forms of financial aid and to complete any necessary applications.

2. **Maximize Free Resources**: Take advantage of free resources and opportunities to minimize college costs. For emphasis, we're bringing this back to the table. Consider Advanced Placement (AP) or dual enrollment courses in high school to earn college credits. Additionally, explore participation in community service activities that may qualify you for scholarships.

3. **Consider Community College**: Starting your college journey at a community college can be a cost-effective way to earn college credits and fulfill general education requirements before transferring to a four-year institution. Community colleges often have lower tuition rates than four-year colleges and universities, making them a more affordable option for many students.

4. **Explore Tuition Assistance Programs**: Some employers offer tuition assistance programs to benefit their employees. If you're working part-time or full-time while attending college, check with your employer to see if they offer any tuition assistance or reimbursement programs.

5. **Compare Financial Aid Packages**: When evaluating college options, compare financial aid packages from different schools to determine which offers the best combination of scholarships, grants, and loans. Consider factors like total cost of attendance, average student loan debt, and graduation rates when making your decision.

6. **Budget Wisely**: Create a budget for your college expenses and stick to it. Be mindful of your spending and prioritize your needs over your wants. Look for ways to save money on textbooks, housing, transportation, and other expenses to stretch your financial resources further.

Maximizing your financial resources while minimizing the burden of student debt is very achievable. With careful planning, diligence, and making informed decisions, you'll be well on your way to achieving your college dreams without breaking the bank.

Budgeting for Life Transitions

Hey there, future adults! Ready to navigate the dynamic pathway of life's exciting adulting journey? Get ready to tackle major life transitions like a boss, armed with the financial savvy to navigate the ups and downs with confidence.

Preparing for Major Life Transitions

As you prepare to embark on major life transitions, such as starting a career, moving out on your own, or getting married, it's important to be financially prepared for the road ahead. Let's break down the financial implications of these life changes and how to adjust your budget accordingly.

1. **Starting a Career**: Landing your first job or starting a career is like stepping onto a new stage—it's exciting, nerve-wracking, and full of potential. But with a steady paycheck comes new financial responsibilities, and in a career, there could be enormous challenges, especially in the early stages. You'll need to budget for essentials like rent, utilities, groceries, transportation, and healthcare expenses. Consider setting up automatic transfers to your savings account to build an emergency fund and save for future goals. And don't forget about retirement—even though it may seem far off, starting to save early can have a big impact on your financial future.

2. **Moving Out on Your Own**: Moving out of your parent's house is like spreading your wings and taking flight into

the great unknown. It's a grand adventure that's liberating. But before you soar, you'll need to make sure your financial nest is in order because it comes with its fair share of challenges. Factor in expenses like rent, utilities, groceries, transportation, and insurance when creating your budget. Consider sharing living expenses with roommates to reduce costs and exploring ways to save money on rent, such as living in a more affordable neighborhood or negotiating with landlords.

3. **Getting Married**: Tying the knot with your soulmate is like joining forces in a lifelong quest for happiness—it's a beautiful journey to conquer the world together, but it also requires careful planning and financial teamwork. Love and happiness come from shared financial responsibilities. You'll need to budget for wedding expenses like venue rental, catering, attire, and entertainment. But this isn't even where the work is!

After the wedding bells stopped ringing, the real work began. You'll need to adjust your budget to accommodate expenses like rent, utilities, groceries, and shared financial goals. Communication is key—sit down with your partner and make sure to have open and honest conversations about your financial situations (income, debts, and savings), priorities, goals, and expectations.

Aside from your personal accounts, you can consider creating a joint budget that reflects your combined income and expenses and establishing shared financial goals like buying a home or saving for retirement. Be honest and work together to build a solid financial foundation for your future together.

Financial Implications of Life Changes and How to Adjust Budgets Accordingly

As a teenage financial expert, you're well aware at this stage that life can be highly unpredictable sometimes. Right? So, let's talk about adjusting your budget to accommodate these life changes. It's like tuning your instrument to play a new song—you'll need to fine-tune your budget to accommodate changes in income, expenses, and financial goals.

As your circumstances change, like starting a new job or moving to a new city, reassess your budget and make adjustments as needed to ensure your financial goals remain on track.

For example, if you're starting a new job with a higher salary, consider increasing your savings contributions or paying down debt more aggressively. You could embark on reallocating funds from nonessential categories to cover new expenses or look for ways to increase your income through side hustles or career advancement opportunities. If you're moving to a new city with a higher cost of living, look for ways to reduce expenses and prioritize your needs over your wants. And if you're getting married, merge your individual budgets into a joint budget that reflects your shared financial goals and priorities.

You can embark on adulthood with confidence and resilience. Embrace the journey, plan carefully, make smart financial decisions, stay flexible, and remember—with a solid budget and a positive mindset, you can conquer anything life throws your way!

Do well to internalize these powerful quotes below:

> *"It does not do to leave a live dragon out of your calculations, if you live near one."*

J.R.R. Tolkien (Hughes, 2018)

"Give me six hours to chop down a tree and I will spend the first four sharpening the axe."

Abraham Lincoln (Hughes, 2018)

"By Failing to prepare, you are preparing to fail."

Benjamin Franklin (Hughes, 2018)

Interactive Element

Hey, check out this budgeting simulator below. You'll like it. No shill.

Jump$tart's Reality Check: https://www.jumpstart.org/what-we-do/support-financial-education/reality-check/.

This is a budgeting simulator where you can input your financial goals, expenses, and income to simulate budgeting for major life events such as college expenses, moving out, or buying a home. This interactive tool allows you to experiment with different scenarios and make informed financial decisions in a risk-free environment.

Simply put, "Reality Check" is a way to see into your future based on the intended lifestyle for your future, the kind of career you intend to pursue, and other factors that just form the way you intend to live ($tart, 2023).

It reinforces the concepts discussed in the chapter and enhances your understanding of financial planning for significant milestones.

As we wrap up this chapter on "Planning for Major Life Events," it's crucial to reflect on the significance of the insights and strategies we've discussed. Throughout the F.I.N.A.N.C.E. Blueprint, we've emphasized the importance of preparing for life's transitions with careful planning, resilience, and adaptability.

These insights and strategies aren't just isolated tactics—they're integral components of the F.I.N.A.N.C.E. Blueprint, guiding you on a path toward financial independence and empowerment. As you continue on your financial journey, remember that each decision you make, each budget you create, and each goal you set brings you one step closer to achieving your dreams and building a secure future for yourself.

Now, as we turn the page to the next chapter, we're embarking on a transformative journey into the realm of giving back and philanthropy. Just as you've learned to manage your own finances responsibly, it's time to embrace your role as a financial steward and champion of positive change in your community and beyond. Through the power of giving back, you have the opportunity to make a meaningful impact on the world around you, leaving a legacy that extends far beyond your own lifetime. So, let's dive into the next chapter with open hearts and open minds, ready to explore the transformative power of philanthropy and discover how we can all make a difference, one act of kindness at a time. Together, we can create a brighter, more equitable future for ourselves and generations to come. Are you ready to be a part of something bigger than yourself? Let's make a difference together!

Interactive Questions

1 .When budgeting for college expenses, which of the following factors should you consider?

a) Only tuition fees
b) Only housing expenses
c) Both tuition fees and housing expenses
d) None of the above
e) Only transportation costs

2. What is one strategic tip for minimizing college costs?

a) Taking out multiple loans
b) Researching financial aid options early
c) Not applying for scholarships
d) Ignoring budgeting altogether
e) Not considering community college as an option

3. When budgeting for moving out on your own, what should you budget for?

a) Only rent
b) Only groceries
c) Both rent and groceries
d) Only entertainment expenses
e) Only travel expenses

Fascinating Facts

1. The concept of credit dates back to ancient civilizations

like Mesopotamia, where merchants would extend credit to farmers for crops.

2. The first paper money in the United States was issued by the Massachusetts Bay Colony in 1690.

3. The average American household spends over $1,000 per year on coffee.

4. The concept of insurance dates back to ancient China, where merchants would distribute their goods across multiple ships to minimize losses from shipwrecks.

5. The New York Stock Exchange (NYSE) is the largest in the world, with a market capitalization of over $30 trillion.

6. The world's first ATM (Automated Teller Machine) was installed in 1967 by Barclays Bank in London.

7. The average lifetime earnings of a college graduate are significantly higher than those of someone with only a high school diploma.

NINE

Giving Back and Philanthropy

Are you ready to make a positive impact on the world while managing your finances responsibly? This chapter dives into the transformative power of giving back and incorporating philanthropy into your financial plans.

Understanding the Value of Giving

Hey there, future changemakers! Get ready to explore the transformative power of giving back and making a positive impact on the world around you. In this subchapter, we'll delve into why giving back is so important and the incredible benefits it brings to both individuals and communities.

Importance of Giving Back to the Community

Picture this: You're walking down the street, and you see someone in need. Maybe it's a neighbor struggling to put food on the table or a local organization raising funds for a worthy cause. In that moment, you have the opportunity to make a difference—to lend a helping hand and be a force for good in the world.

But why is giving back so important? Let's break it down.

1. **Personal Growth**: Giving back isn't just about helping others—it's also about personal growth and fulfillment. When you give back, you experience a sense of purpose and satisfaction that comes from making a positive impact on the lives of others. It's like watering a plant and watching it bloom—by nurturing your spirit of generosity. You cultivate a sense of joy and fulfillment that enriches your own life as well as the lives of those around you.

2. **Social Responsibility**: As members of society, we all have a responsibility to contribute to the common good and help create a more equitable and compassionate world. Giving back is like paying it forward—sharing your time, talents, and resources with others. When you engage in causes like this, you're investing in the well-being of your community and fostering a sense of solidarity and interconnectedness that transcends boundaries and differences.

3. **Building Strong Communities**: When individuals come together to support one another, amazing things happen. Giving back strengthens the fabric of our communities, creating a network of support and compassion that uplifts everyone. It's like building a bridge. Connecting with others and working toward a common goal creates a stronger, more resilient community that can weather any storm.

Benefits of Philanthropy for Personal Growth, Social Responsibility, and Building Strong Communities

Now, let's talk about the incredible benefits of philanthropy for personal growth, social responsibility, and building strong communities:

When you give back, you develop valuable skills like empathy, compassion, and leadership that serve you well in all areas of your life. Whether you're volunteering at a local food bank, organizing a charity fundraiser, or donating to a worthy cause, you're honing your ability to connect with others and make a positive impact on the world.

Furthermore, while giving back, you demonstrate your commitment to creating a more just and equitable society where everyone has the opportunity to thrive. Whether you're advocating for social justice, supporting environmental conservation efforts, or volunteering your time and talents to help those in need, you're contributing to the greater good and inspiring others to do the same.

Moreover, philanthropy strengthens the bonds that hold our communities together, creating a sense of belonging and mutual support that benefits everyone. Whether you're volunteering with your neighbors to clean up a local park, donating to a community development project, or supporting small businesses in your area, you're investing in the well-being of your community and helping to create a brighter future for everyone.

Exploring Different Ways to Give Back – Volunteering Time, Donating Money, and Advocacy

Hey there, future changemakers! Now that we understand the value of giving back let's explore some practical ways you can get involved and make a difference in your community and beyond. Whether you're passionate about helping people, protecting the environment, or advocating for social justice, there's something for everyone to do to contribute to positive change.

1. **Volunteering Time**: Volunteering your time is like planting seeds of kindness that can grow into a forest of goodwill. There are countless ways to get involved in your community, from helping out at a local soup kitchen or animal shelter to tutoring students or participating in neighborhood clean-up events. Consider your interests, skills, and availability, and find a volunteer opportunity that aligns with your passions and values. For example, if you love animals, you could volunteer at a local animal shelter, helping to care for and socialize rescued pets. Or, if you're passionate about the environment, you could join a beach clean-up crew or participate in tree-planting initiatives to help protect natural habitats.

2. **Donating Money**: Donating money is like fueling the engines of change—it provides the resources needed to support important causes and make a meaningful impact. Whether you're donating a few dollars or a larger sum, every contribution counts and can make a difference in the lives of others. Consider supporting organizations and charities that align with your values and interests, whether it's providing food and shelter for the homeless, funding medical research, or supporting education initiatives. For example, if you're passionate about ending hunger, you could donate to a local food bank or community pantry, helping to provide meals for families in need. Or, if you're concerned about climate change, you could donate to an environmental organization working to protect and preserve our planet for future generations.

3. **Advocating for Causes**: Advocating for causes you believe in is like raising your voice to create positive change in the world. Whether you're speaking out on social media, writing letters to elected officials, or organizing rallies and protests, advocacy is a powerful way to raise awareness,

mobilize support, and influence policy decisions. Consider issues that are important to you, whether it's racial justice, political responsibility, gender rights, or access to healthcare, and find ways to advocate for change. For example, if you're passionate about environmental conservation, you could join a local climate action group and participate in advocacy campaigns to promote renewable energy and protect endangered species. Or, if you're concerned about gun violence, you could organize a student-led march or rally to demand stronger gun control measures and safer communities.

Dear teen changemaker, explore different ways to give back. You have the power to make a meaningful impact and create positive change in the world. Find what moves you, get involved, and let your light shine bright as you make a difference in the lives of others!

Are you ready to be a force for good? Let's make a difference together!

Incorporating Philanthropy into Financial Planning

Hey there, compassionate teens! Now that we've discussed the importance of giving back let's talk about how you can incorporate philanthropy into your financial planning and make a meaningful impact on the causes you care about. Whether you're passionate about animal welfare, environmental conservation, or supporting education initiatives, there are plenty of ways to give back while managing your finances responsibly.

Incorporating Charitable Giving into Financial Plans and Budgets

Just like budgeting for groceries or saving for a rainy day, incorporating charitable giving into your financial plan is a smart way to prioritize your values and make a difference in the world. Consider setting aside a portion of your income or allowance each month for charitable donations. For example, you could designate a certain percentage of your earnings to support a cause you care about, whether it's donating to a local animal shelter, supporting a community food bank, or funding medical research. Making charitable giving a regular part of your budget helps ensure that you're able to support important causes while still meeting your financial goals.

Strategies for Maximizing the Impact of Charitable Donations

Want to make your charitable dollars go even further? There are plenty of strategies you can use to maximize the impact of your donations and ensure that your money is making a meaningful difference in the world. One option is to take advantage of employer matching programs, where your employer matches your charitable donations up to a certain amount. For example, if you donate $100 to a charitable organization, your employer may match that donation with an additional $100, doubling the impact of your gift.

Another strategy is to set up a donor-advised fund, which allows you to make a charitable contribution and receive an immediate tax deduction while also retaining the ability to recommend how the funds are distributed to charitable organizations over time. When you employ these strategies, you can amplify the impact of your charitable giving and make a lasting difference in the lives of others.

Let's consider a scenario: Kerene is passionate about helping homeless youth in her community. She decides to incorporate charitable giving into her monthly budget by setting aside $50 from her part-time job earnings to donate to a local youth shelter. To maximize the impact of her donation, Kerene checks with her employer and discovers that they offer a matching program for charitable contributions. She submits her donation to the youth shelter, and her employer matches her gift, doubling the amount of support for homeless youth in her community. Through thoughtful financial planning and strategic giving, Kerene is able to make a meaningful impact on a cause she cares about while managing her finances responsibly.

So think about what matters most to you, set aside some funds for charitable giving, and watch as your generosity transforms lives and communities for the better!

Becoming Thoughtful and Intentional Philanthropists – Aligning Giving with Values and Priorities

Hey there, compassionate teens! As we near the end of our journey into the world of giving back and philanthropy, it's time to reflect on how you can become thoughtful and intentional philanthropists, making a meaningful impact on the causes you care about while also aligning your giving with your values and priorities.

Imagine this: You have the power to change the world with your generosity and compassion. Whether you're passionate about protecting the environment, fighting for social justice, or supporting education initiatives, your contributions can make a real difference in the lives of others and create positive change in the world.

So, how can you become a thoughtful and intentional philanthropist? Here are a few tips to get you started:

1. **Identify Your Values and Priorities**: Take some time to reflect on what matters most to you and what causes you're passionate about. Whether it's helping animals, empowering underserved communities, or advocating for equality and justice, your values and priorities will guide your philanthropic efforts and ensure that your giving is meaningful and impactful.

2. **Do Your Research**: Once you've identified your values and priorities, take the time to research organizations and charities that align with your interests. Look for organizations that have a proven track record of making a positive impact in their respective fields and are transparent about how they use donor funds. Consider reaching out to local nonprofits or community organizations to learn more about their work and how you can get involved.

3. **Be Strategic in Your Giving**: Just like budgeting for your own expenses, it's important to be strategic in your philanthropic giving. Consider how you can maximize the impact of your donations by leveraging employer matching programs, setting up donor-advised funds, or exploring other giving vehicles that align with your financial goals and objectives.

So, as you take these final steps in your financial journey, remember that generosity is a powerful force for good, and each act of kindness has the potential to create ripple effects that extend far beyond your own life. Incorporating philanthropy into your financial plan not only makes you a contributor to a positive impact on the world, but it also shapes a well-rounded financial perspective that prioritizes giving back and making a difference.

One icon to learn from in this regard is LeBron James, a basketball legend known for his incredible skills on the court and his philanthropic efforts off the court (Adams, 2023). LeBron has used his platform to promote financial literacy and empower underserved communities to build brighter futures. His commitment to financial education has inspired countless individuals to take control of their financial destinies and pursue their dreams.

Here's what he said:

"I told myself if I ever made it to the level I am, I'm gonna give back."

(Quotes, 2024)

Interactive Element

Hey, check out this amazing philanthropy toolkit. It's a valuable resource that guides you through the process of planning your charitable giving, helping you set goals, allocate funds, and track your impact over time.

The Stanford PACS Philanthropy Toolkit: https://pacscenter.stanford.edu/the-philanthropy-toolkit/.

The toolkit is a practical step-by-step resource designed to help you, your family, and your advisors engage in thoughtful conversations, be effective in your charitable giving, and anchor your philanthropy around what most deeply inspires you.

Here's a breakdown of what this toolkit helps you do:

- Find your unique focus areas based on your motivation and values.
- Seek professional advice and engage family and other communities or groups
- Structure your giving.
- Find and vet organizations.
- Make gifts and track your giving (PACS, 2024).

Now, let's tie it all back to the overarching principles of the F.I.N.A.N.C.E. Blueprint. Throughout our journey, we've emphasized the importance of responsible financial management, strategic planning, and thoughtful decision-making. It's been an amazing ride till this point—one that's involved pouring out all that's relevant to make you fully equipped to soar financially.

It's now time to transition seamlessly to the conclusion, where we'll reflect on the insights and skills gained throughout this journey and create a comprehensive financial plan for a prosperous future. Let's go this last mile together!

Interactive Questions

1. What is one benefit of incorporating charitable giving into your financial plan?

   a) Increased spending on personal luxuries
   b) Greater financial stability
   c) Higher credit card debt
   d) Lower savings rate
   e) None of the above

2. How can you maximize the impact of your charitable donations?

    a) Avoid donating altogether
    b) Use donor-advised funds
    c) Ignore employer matching programs
    d) Give sporadically without a plan
    e) None of the above

3. What is an example of aligning giving with values and priorities?

    a) Donating randomly to any charity
    b) Volunteering without purpose
    c) Supporting environmental conservation if passionate about it
    d) Giving to a charity without knowing what it does
    e) None of the above

Fascinating Facts

1. The world's first ATM was installed in 1967 by Barclays Bank in London.
2. The largest bill ever printed by the U.S. Treasury was the $100,000 bill, which featured President Woodrow Wilson and was used only for transactions between Federal Reserve Banks.
3. The average millionaire has seven streams of income.
4. The concept of paper money dates back to ancient China, where merchants used "flying cash" certificates as early as the 7th century.

5. The most expensive coin ever sold was a 1794 Flowing Hair Silver Dollar, which fetched over $10 million at auction.

6. In 2010, a programmer paid for two pizzas with 10,000 bitcoins. At today's value, those bitcoins would be worth over $500 million.

7. The first credit card called the Diners Club card, was introduced in 1950 and could only be used at twenty-seven restaurants in New York City.

Conclusion

Money Skills for Teen Blueprint empowers teenagers to take control of their financial futures through clear guidance, practical strategies, and actionable tips. By gaining mastery in essential money skills like budgeting, saving, and smart spending, readers gain the confidence and clarity needed to achieve financial independence and build a solid foundation for future success.

Having reached this stage of our journey through *Money Skills for Teen Blueprint*, it's time to reflect on the key lessons we've learned and the powerful principles that will shape our financial futures. Throughout this book, we've covered a wide range of topics. Now, let's bring it all together and reinforce the key principles of the F.I.N.A.N.C.E. Blueprint.

F – Foundation Building: We've emphasized the importance of laying a strong foundation for financial success by mastering the basics of money management, budgeting, and credit. Understanding these fundamental concepts provides you with the necessary tools to make informed decisions and build a secure financial future.

I – Investment in Education: We've established that investing in your education isn't just about getting good grades. It involves an intentional pursuit of the right knowledge that would buffer your finances. We've explored various financial concepts, from stocks and bonds to banking services and the power of early investing for long-term wealth accumulation. Having familiarized yourself with various financial concepts and the importance of investing early for long-term wealth accumulation, you're setting yourself up for success and prosperity.

N – Nurture Smart Spending Habits: Smart spending isn't about depriving yourself of the things you enjoy—it's about making thoughtful choices that align with your financial goals. It's about distinguishing between needs and wants, prioritizing spending on essentials, and allocating discretionary funds wisely. These ideas make it easy to live within your means and achieve your financial dreams.

A – Assess and Adapt Budgeting Skills: We've learned that budgeting isn't a one-time task—it's an ongoing process that requires regular assessment and adjustment. It involves equipping yourself with practical budgeting techniques and regularly reviewing your income and expenses to help you stay on track to meet your financial goals and adapt to changing circumstances.

N – Navigate Borrowing and Debt: You can agree that borrowing money isn't inherently bad—it's how you manage it that matters. You've been better positioned to understand the implications of borrowing and debt. By practicing responsible borrowing practices, you can avoid debt traps and maintain financial stability.

C – Cultivate Savings Mindset: Saving money isn't just about stashing cash under your mattress—it's about setting goals, making sacrifices, and planning for the future. It involves cultivating a savings mindset and harnessing the power of compound interest to help you build a financial safety net and achieve your long-term goals.

E – Empowerment through Action: Finally, we've noted that it's time to take action and apply the knowledge and skills you've gained to shape your financial future. Seek opportunities to earn, save, invest, and make informed financial decisions. This way, you can take charge of your financial destiny and create the life you want.

As we close the chapter on *Money Skills for Teen Blueprint*, let's take a moment to celebrate the transformative journey we've embarked upon together and share the profound impact it has had on the lives of teens like you. Allow me to introduce you to Meyers, a remarkable teenager who applied the principles of the F.I.N.A.N.C.E. Blueprint and witnessed remarkable changes in her financial habits and mindset.

Before discovering the F.I.N.A.N.C.E. Blueprint, Meyers found herself constantly struggling to make ends meet. Like many teens, she didn't have a clear understanding of basic financial concepts and often found herself spending her allowance impulsively without much thought for the future. She dreamed of a brighter future but felt trapped by her lack of financial knowledge and the cycle of paycheck-to-paycheck living.

But everything changed when Meyers stumbled upon *Money Skills for Teen Blueprint*. From the very first page, she was captivated by the clear and concise explanations of financial concepts explicitly tailored to teenagers like her. Finally, she found a resource that spoke her language and addressed her unique needs and challenges.

Armed with practical strategies and actionable tips gleaned from the book, Meyers set out to take control of her finances like never before. She learned how to budget wisely, track her expenses, and save money for future goals. No longer did she feel overwhelmed by the complexities of personal finance—instead, she felt empowered to navigate them with confidence and clarity.

One of the most significant changes Meyers experienced was in her spending habits. Before, she would often splurge on unnecessary purchases without considering the long-term consequences. But now, she approached spending with a newfound sense of mindfulness, distinguishing between needs and wants and making informed decisions about where to allocate her funds.

Through the guidance of *Money Skills for Teen Blueprint*, Meyers built a solid financial foundation for future success. She learned the importance of setting financial goals, creating an emergency fund, and investing in her future through smart savings and investing strategies. With each passing day, she felt more confident and empowered to take charge of her financial destiny.

However, perhaps the most profound impact of all was the sense of empowerment Meyers gained from reading this book. No longer did she feel like a victim of her circumstances—instead, she felt like a master of her own destiny, capable of achieving anything she set her mind to. With the valuable resources and tools provided in the book, she streamlined her learning process and gained the knowledge and skills needed to thrive in today's complex financial landscape.

As Meyers looks back on her journey, she can't help but feel grateful for stumbling upon *Money Skills for Teen Blueprint*. What started as a simple desire to improve her financial literacy has blossomed into a journey of self-discovery and empowerment. Thanks to this book, Meyers is no longer held back by her financial limitations—instead, she's propelled forward by the boundless possibilities that lie ahead.

So, to all the teens out there reading this book, take heart—you're not alone on this journey. With the F.I.N.A.N.C.E. Blueprint as your guide, you have everything you need to unleash wealth and financial sustainability in your life. Embracing these principles and applying them in your daily life means you're not only building wealth—you're also building a well-rounded financial perspective that will serve you well for years to come. And lest this slips off, do well to share what you've learned with friends and family, spreading the knowledge and fostering a culture of financial responsibility in your community. So go forth, savvy teens, and seize the opportunities that lie ahead. With the F.I.N.A.N.C.E. Blueprint as your guide, your brighter future awaits. The sky's the limit!

Keeping the Game Alive

Congratulations! You now have all the tools you need to unlock financial independence. But there's one more thing you can do to keep the momentum going—share your knowledge.

By leaving your honest opinion of this book on Amazon, you'll guide other Teens to the resources they need to start their journey toward smart money management.

Your review helps spread the passion for Money Skills and keeps this valuable knowledge alive. Just scan the QR code below to leave your feedback and help others find their way:

Thank you for your help. Together, we're keeping the spirit of Money Skills for Teens alive and thriving!

These pages are crafted to encourage readers to share their experience and help spread the knowledge contained within "Money Skills for Teens Blueprints," emphasizing community support and the personal growth that comes from helping others.

References

Adeodun, Adenike. 2023. "Jay Z: How a Brooklyn Boy Became a Billionaire Mogul." *Billionaires. Africa.* November 14. https://billionaires.africa/2023/11/14/jay-z-how-a-brooklyn-boy-became-a-billionaire-mogul/.

Andrews, Eve. 2024. "What Ever Happened to the Tiny House Movement?" *Wired.* https://www.wired.com/story/what-ever-happened-to-the-tiny-house-movement/.

Badenhausen, Kurt. 2024. "Inside Serena Williams' Plan To Ace Venture Investing." *Forbes.* 10. https://www.forbes.com/sites/kurtbadenhausen/2019/06/03/inside-serena-williams-plan-to-ace-venture-investing/.

Batdorf, Emily. 2023. "Savings Goal Calculator – Forbes Advisor." *Forbes Advisor.* June 27. https://www.forbes.com/advisor/banking/savings/savings-goal-calculator/.

"Best Financial Apps for Teens and Young Adults." 2018. *SageVest Kids.* December 11. https://www.kidsfinancialeducation.com/best-financial-apps-for-teens-and-young-adults/.

Coblentz, Emilee. 2024. "'No Minimum Age to Start': Illinois Teen Says Investing Young Allowed Her to Buy Tesla." *USA TODAY.* March 1. https://www.usatoday.com/story/money/2024/03/01/young-investor-sophia-castiblanco/72760552007/.

"Dave Ramsey Quote: 'A Budget Is Telling Your Money Where to Go Instead of Wondering Where It Went.'" 2024. 10. https://quotefancy.com/quote/1377713/Dave-Ramsey-A-budget-is-telling-your-money-where-to-go-instead-of-wondering-where-it-went.

Division X Technical Assistance. 2023. "Providing Direct Financial Assistance to Youth and Young Adults." *Child Welfare Capacity Building Collaborative.* https://capacity.childwelfare.gov/states/resources/financial-assistance-youth.

"Do Not Save What Is Left After Spending, Spend What Is Left After Saving." 2023. *Kotak Securities.* February 21. https://www.kotaksecurities.com/articles/do-not-save-what-is-left-after-spending-spend-what-is-left-after-saving/.

Editorial Desk. 2023. "History of Budget." *The Business Post.* June 2. https://businesspostbd.com/opinion-todays-paper/2023-06-02/history-of-budget-2023-06-02.

Editors. 2023. "LeBron James: Two Decades of Dominance on and off the Court | Editorial – The Daily Free Press." October 31. https://dailyfreepress.com/2023/

10/31/lebron-james-two-decades-of-dominance-on-and-off-the-court-editorial/.

Entrepreneur Daily. 2014. "6 Stories of Super Successes Who Overcame Failure." *Entrepreneur*. December 8. https://www.entrepreneur.com/leadership/6-stories-of-super-successes-who-overcame-failure/240492.

Family Finance. 2023. "Einstein's Compound Interest - The 8th Wonder of the World - Greatest Gift." *Greatest Gift*. December 25. https://www.greatestgiftapp.com/blog/einstein-compound-interest.

Heidi. 2021. "12 Online Financial Resources for Teens." *StartsAtEight*. October 5. https://www.startsateight.com/online-financial-resources-for-teens/.

Her Agenda. 2024. "Life After Tennis: Serena Williams Is A Force In Venture Capital." *Her Agenda*. March 19. https://heragenda.com/p/serena-williams-venture-capital-firm/.

"How the Founder of Mo's Bows Tapped Into His Dream at a Young Age." 2019. *U.S. Chamber of Commerce*. October 21. https://www.uschamber.com/co/good-company/growth-studio/mos-bows-founder-moziah-bridges.

Hughes, Kris. 2018. "25 of the Best Planning Quotes." *ProjectManager*. October 4. https://www.projectmanager.com/blog/planning-quotes.

James, LeBron. 2024. "LeBron James Quotes About Giving." *A-Z Quotes*. https://www.azquotes.com/author/7332-LeBron_James/tag/giving.

Kamel, George. 2024. "10 Best Ways to Save for College." *Ramsey Solutions*. https://www.ramseysolutions.com/saving/saving-for-college-is-easier-than-you-think.

Konrad, Alex. 2024. "How Super Angel Chris Sacca Made Billions, Burned Bridges and Crafted The Best Seed Portfolio Ever." *Forbes*. https://www.forbes.com/sites/alexkonrad/2015/03/25/how-venture-cowboy-chris-sacca-made-billions/.

Kusimba, Chapurukha. 2017. "When – and Why – Did People First Start Using Money?" *The Conversation*. June 20. http://theconversation.com/when-and-why-did-people-first-start-using-money-78887.

Lake, Sydney. 2024. "Spanx Founder Sara Blakely's $1 Billion Idea Started with Just $5,000 in Savings and Wanting to Solve Her Own Problem." *Fortune*. https://fortune.com/2024/02/27/sara-blakely-spanx-billion-dollar-idea-oprah-5000-savings-billionaire/.

Lew, Jack. n.d. "The Budget Is Not Just a Collection of Numbers, but an Expression of Our Values and Aspirations." *BrainyQuote*. https://www.brainyquote.com/quotes/jack_lew_442942.

Lewis, Finley. 2024. "9 Rules to Dominate Your Money and Learn What 67% Of Adults Don't Know." *Finley Lewis*. https://www.finleylewis.com.

Lovett, Johnnie. 2024. "SAVING EARLY: KEY TO SUCCESSFUL

FUTURE." *AmericaSaves*. https://americasaves.org/resource-center/saver-tips-and-stories/saving-early-key-to-successful-future/.

Matt. 2023. "Piñatex Pineapple Leather: The Fascinating Story of Transforming Waste into Fashion." *Rahui London*. October 1. https://www.rahui.com/blogs/vegan-leather-types/pinatex-pineapple-leather.

McNay, Shannon. 2017. "5 Inspiring Stories of People Paying off Thousands in Student Loans and Still Winning at Life." *CNBC*. June 28. https://www.cnbc.com/2017/06/28/5-inspiring-stories-of-people-paying-off-thousands-in-student-loans.html.

"More Plastic Than Fish." 2024. *Plastic Soup Foundation*. https://www.plasticsoupfoundation.org/en/plastic-problem/plastic-soup/more-plastic-than-fish/.

Palmer, Kimberly. 2015. "Why Teen Savers Have More Financial Success Later in Life." *Yahoo News*. September 9. http://news.yahoo.com/why-teen-savers-more-financial-success-later-life-141135263.html.

"Reality Check – Online Tool for Students." 2024. *Jump$tart Coalition*. https://www.jumpstart.org/education/reality-check/.

Rohn, Jim. n.d. "Discipline Is the Bridge between Goals and Accomplishment." *BrainyQoute*. https://www.brainyquote.com/quotes/jim_rohn_109882.

Rose, Lylia. 2023. "My £17500 Teenage Debt Story & How To Manage Debt." *Lylia Rose*. May 2. https://www.lyliarose.com/blog/read_203629/my-17500-teenage-debt-story-how-to-manage-debt.html.

Sather, Andrew. 2023. "Quotes from 11 Billionaire Investors about Debt and Finance." *eB*. March 24. https://einvestingforbeginners.com/billionaire-investors-debt-quotes/.

Scott-Briggs, Angela, and Angela Scott-Briggs TechBullion. 2023. "Successful Teenage Investor Shares Financial Secrets for Teens." *TechBullion*. August 26. https://techbullion.com/successful-teenage-investor-shares-financial-secrets-for-teens/.

Simon-Gersuk, Carly. 2024. "Five Financial Literacy Organizations You Should Know About." *MoveCU*. https://movecu.com/blogs/5-financial-literacy-organizations-you-should-know-about.

Tearle, Dr. Oliver. 2021. "The Meaning and Origins of 'Neither a Borrower Nor a Lender Be'?" *Interesting Literature*. June 16. https://interestingliterature.com/2021/06/neither-a-borrower-nor-a-lender-be-meaning-origins-analysis/.

"Teen Budget Calculator." 2022. *MoneyFit*. May 18. https://www.moneyfit.org/budget-calculator-for-teens/.

"The Philanthropy Toolkit." 2024. *Stanford PACS*. https://pacscenter.stanford.edu/the-philanthropy-toolkit/.

Thunberg, Greta. 2019. "Greta Thunberg: Who Is the Climate Activist and What Has She Achieved?" *BBC*. November 29. https://www.bbc.com/news/world-europe-49918719.

"Tools and Resources for Introducing Kids to Money Management." 2022. *SageVest Kids*. June 13. https://www.kidsfinancialeducation.com/tools-and-resources-for-introducing-kids-to-money-management/.

Tretina, Kat. 2023. "Types of College Funds for Kids." *USA TODAY Blueprint*. February 10. https://www.usatoday.com/money/blueprint/investing/college-funds-for-kids/.

Tretina, Kat, and Alicia Hahn. 2021. "13 Companies That Pay Your Student Loans – Forbes Advisor." *Forbes Advisor*. November 19. https://www.forbes.com/advisor/student-loans/companies-that-pay-student-loans/?utm_medium=social&utm_campaign=socialflowForbesMainTwitter&utm_source=ForbesMainTwitter.

Turner, Terry. 2023. "47+ Fascinating Financial Literacy Statistics in 2023." *Annuity.Org*. December 7. https://www.annuity.org/financial-literacy/financial-literacy-statistics/.

Ziglar, Zig. n.d. "Be Careful Not to Compromise What You Want Most for What You Want Now." *BrainyQuote*. https://www.brainyquote.com/quotes/zig_ziglar_617765.